the **impatient**
patchworker

the **impatient** patchworker

jayne emerson

PHOTOGRAPHS BY **JOHN HESELTINE**

POTTER
CRAFT

New York

Copyright © 2006 by Rowan Yarns
Text and design copyright © 2006 by Jayne Emerson

All rights reserved.
Published in the United States by Potter Craft, an imprint of
the Crown Publishing Group, a division of Random House, Inc.,
New York.
www.crownpublishing.com
www.clarksonpotter.com

Originally published in Great Britain by Rowan Yarns,
West Yorkshire, in 2006.

Potter Craft and Clarkson N. Potter are trademarks
and Potter and colophon are registered trademarks, of
Random House, Inc.

Library of Congress Cataloging-in-Publication Data is
available upon request.

ISBN 13: 978-0-307-33657-6
ISBN 10: 0-307-33657-3

Printed in Singapore

Project editor and stylist Susan Berry
Editor Sally Harding
Designer Anne Wilson
Illustrations Carrie Hill
Photographer John Heseltine

10 9 8 7 6 5 4 3 2 1

First American Edition

contents

introduction

Some might say that the words "patchwork" and "impatient" do not go together, but they are mistaken. Modern patchwork has been greatly advanced by the invention of rotary cutters and cutting mats, and it is now possible to make an entire quilt in a weekend. This, however, is still too much time if you want an instant creation, so I have designed a collection of projects that exemplify patchwork and can be made in a matter of hours.

Patchwork has become very fashionable, and vintage quilts are highly sought-after commodities. People began making patchwork to use up fabric scraps, and there is no reason why this tradition should not continue. We live in such a throwaway society that reusing fabric remnants and favorite old dresses can become a wonderful way to recycle.

It is very satisfying to be able to make something that is uniquely personal for yourself or someone else. I love the practice of patchworking small items for the home and turning everyday objects into beautiful and precious keepsakes.

This book has all kinds of things for you to stitch, from makeup and tote bags to tablecloths, cushions, and runners. Although the patchwork projects are mostly for small accessories like those, if you become more interested in the craft, it would be very easy to enlarge these designs to make bigger ones. For example, the cushions on page 70 could be turned effortlessly into a quilt design, and the table runner alternative on page 69 would make a great duvet cover.

If you make large patchwork pieces composed of two layers of fabric with batting between them, you will need to stitch the batting in place through all the layers (a process called "quilting"). The basic principles for quilting are explained on pages 23–25, just in case. Of course, you do not have to quilt small items, so if you are truly impatient, you can simply skip this section.

Even though these projects are quick and fairly straightforward, you will be disappointed with your patchwork if you don't spend a little time giving them a professional-looking finish, and there are no shortcuts to good results. That said, you will see that I have used several stripe combinations in this book because stripes provide a handy cutting and stitching guide and will help you achieve neat and even sewing.

When I designed these projects, I used Rowan's marvelous range of patchwork fabrics (see pages 108 and 109). Although not all their colorways and prints stay in stock forever, Rowan brings out many new fabrics each season in similar tonal values. You can happily mix and match the old and new fabrics in the same tonal range, or use whatever fabric you prefer.

fabrics

There was a time when all woven fabric was precious. Every salvageable piece of material was used again to make something new, and that's how patchwork was born. Over the centuries, different styles of patchwork have evolved from various cultures, and through them, many stories can be told.

This book is for those who are new to the craft. It is about patchwork in its simplest and most pared-down form. Some of the projects included consist of only two contrasting fabrics; for such projects, the choice of fabrics is more important. A good combination will make a piece that blends comfortably into modern settings.

All the fabrics used in this book are 100 percent pure cotton (see pages 108 and 109). Pure cotton is a great choice for a first-time patchworker—it lasts longer and washes and wears better than other fabrics.

Designed specifically for patchworkers, Rowan fabrics come in a wide range of colors and prints. Although you can substitute the specified fabrics with your own choices, it is wise to stick to the same weight and type of cotton within a single patchwork to ensure a harmonious texture, and to make cutting and stitching easy.

color choices

Color choice is a very personal thing and that, I suppose, is the beauty of patchwork. Sometimes you can put different colors and prints together and they just work. Other times—and this is how I justify such a messy workroom—the discovery that a combination works is the result of a happy happy accident!

Often, the only way to check whether a combination of colors looks right is to collage small pieces of fabrics together before cutting. Stand back and take a good look at the collage; view it from a distance as well as close-up. Fabric colors and prints work very differently when seen from afar. Some blend, others jump out.

I have read many rules and regulations on how to design patchwork, but the truth is that mismatched fabrics and colors give it its unselfconscious charm. You risk losing that

charm, however, if you use many fabrics with patterns that look alike. If one fabric design is too similar to another, it will begin to merge into its neighbor, blurring the patches together. The whole point of patchwork is that it should be a composition of patches and it should not be mistaken for a single cloth print.

That said, there can be times when a merging of color is just what a piece needs, so I have decided that rules are made to be broken, and I will leave you to make up your own!

understanding color values

One of the main points to bear in mind when designing and making patchworks is that color "values" are as important as the colors themselves. These color values, also known as tones, dictate the overall effect of the finished piece. The tone of a color is its lightness or darkness, not to be confused with its actual hue. For most of the projects in this book, I have tended to use rich, medium tones of all colors, but lighter, pastel tones throughout would work equally well.

Experiment with scraps of fabrics, mixing varying amounts of several tones. You will find that some fabrics jump out, while others recede; the key is to get the balance right. Use this art-school trick to discover whether anything jumps out—stand back from your collage and squint your eyes so that your vision is blurry. What you will then see is "tone" rather than "pattern," and you can then easily judge whether one fabric is screaming at you.

Mixing highly contrasting tones within a piece creates the dramatic juxtapositions common in traditional patchwork. The aim of any successful patchwork is to ensure that, whether the contrasts are bold or subtle, the effect of the whole is deliberate. If you are not sure whether a fabric combination works, leave the room for a while. When you come back, you will have a fresh reaction to the design and its effect.

Remember that there are no hard-and-fast rules about combining color values as long as they create a pleasing effect. The important thing is to be happy with the fabric choices before the stitching begins.

mixing prints

To create a feeling of excitement and drama, it often pays to use some large-scale and small-scale prints together to give variety to the design. Or mix different styles of print, such as large-scale florals with neat stripes (see the cushion on page 32 or the runner on page 66). This kind of strong print contrast works very well for asymmetrical patchworks, but would be less successful, obviously, with more traditional styles of even, small patches, such as in the coasters on page 56.

When mixing prints, it pays to have a specific color palette in mind first, limiting the range to perhaps four or five overall colors. This helps unify the design. For the projects in this book, I often offer one or two alternatives for patchworks in different color palettes. Use these suggestions to inspire new color schemes for experiments with your own designs.

Below: The fabrics in the top row demonstrate a medium tone range, and those in the bottom row represent a light tone range. Be careful when mixing light and medium tones, as the paler tones will "jump out." The projects in this book have all been made using the medium tone range.

Using only Rowan fabrics in this book made my life as a patchwork designer easier because each of their fabrics comes in a range of color choices. The opportunity is still there, however, for you to make your own choice of fabrics for any of the projects as long as you bear in mind the color tips on pages 8 and 9.

Also, remember that there are more ways to find fabric than buying it off the roll at the local department store— anything that is discarded and made of cloth can be cut into patches. Garments from thrift stores and rummage sales and even your own unwanted clothes can be cut up as long as the fabric is still in good condition. For professional results, make sure all the fabrics are the same weight, are colorfast, and can be washed at the same temperature.

Opposite: This checkerboard-style cushion (see pages 94–100) is an easy-to-construct, simple-squares patchwork. For this variation, I chose a range of prints and solids in a broadly similar tonal range, so that while the prints and colors differ, the overall effect is unified and elegant. Picking out a principal color for the border is another useful trick for making stylish patchwork designs.

Below: Specially printed patchwork fabrics, such as Rowan's *Swiggle Stripe* below, are ideal because they include several prints in one tonal range in a single length of fabric. You can cut up the fabric to create a variety of different patterns.

Practical fabric tips

There are a few important points to bear in mind before beginning a patchwork.
• Keep your fabrics neatly folded on shelves so that you can see the full range of color choices at your disposal when selecting colorways.
• Always wash your fabrics before starting work on a project. This ensures that the patchwork will not shrink after it has been stitched and that the colors will not bleed. Press the fabric while it is still damp to return it to its original crispness.
• Always use good-quality dressmaker's shears or a sharp rotary cutter (see page 17) for cutting fabrics. Never use fabric scissors for cutting paper: it blunts them with the first cut.
• Cut all your pattern pieces and patches on the straight grain of the fabric unless you are cutting bias strips for edgings. The straight grain of the fabric is either parallel or perpendicular to the selvage, and the bias is at a 45-degree angle to the selvage.
• Cut out all the fabric patches at the beginning and keep them together to use later. If you are using lots of of different fabrics, pin the prints together in groups.

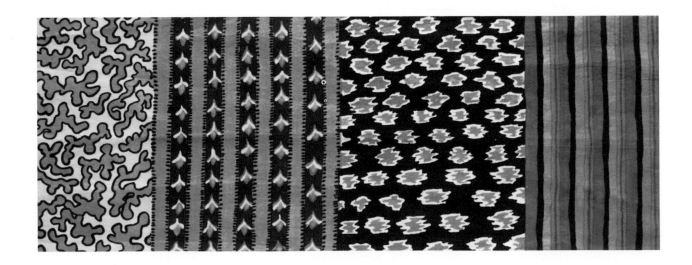

equipment

Even though the patchwork designs in this book are very simple, for satisfying results, it is important to execute them well, with a professional finish. Since they are quick and easy to stitch, you can concentrate on doing a really good job.

To make the process easier and more enjoyable, make sure you have all the right equipment before you start. Assemble everything you need and place it on a special shelf or in a large box. If you are naturally impatient, like me, you may be tempted to ignore this advice. However, there is nothing more annoying than starting on a project and discovering, after the stores have closed, that you don't have an essential piece of equipment.

It is also a good idea to prepare a work space in advance. You will need a large, clean, clear surface and a steam iron and ironing board set up near by. A sewing machine is a must for all but the smallest projects, but nothing fancy is required. I use an old (some would say antique) Singer, which serves me very well. Make sure that you are familiar with the machine, and that you understand how it works. If you haven't used it for a while, take a test run on some fabric scraps. Check that there are extra machine needles in various sizes at hand in case of breakage.

This page lists the equipment you'll need for various tasks. You will probably be able to find many of the items in your general-purpose sewing box. Also, you will not need all of the equipment recommended for every project in the book. For example, only two projects require patchwork templates for drawing patch shapes on fabric (see pages 56–61); the others are made from simple square and rectangular patches, which can be cut without templates.

Choose sewing threads with care. Most fine threads will work for basting. For permanent stitching, if you are working with natural cotton fabric as recommended, use natural cotton thread in matching or toning colors for the best results. Always use a thread that is slightly darker than the fabric because a lighter thread may stand out garishly along the seams.

For quilting, use strong cotton thread that is specially made for quilting. It can be either a boldly contrasting color or one that blends with the fabric.

For preparing patchwork templates
Pencil for tracing and drawing templates
Tracing paper for tracing template shapes
Template seam marker (used in conjunction with a pencil to mark seam allowances around template shapes)
Stiff, thin cardboard or special template plastic for templates
Paper for paper-piecing technique (see page 56–61)
Pair of sharp scissors or craft knife for cutting paper, cardboard, and template plastic

For marking fabric
Tailor's chalk or water-soluble pen or pencil

For cutting fabric
Tape measure and ruler
Pair of sharp dressmaker's shears
Pinking shears (optional)
Rotary cutter (see pages 16 and 17)
Cutting mat
Rectangular plastic rotary-cutter ruler, set square, and metal straight edge or ruler

For stitching
Good sewing machine with basic attachments
Stainless steel pins
Extra-long quilting pins for quilting projects and pinning together padded layers
Pair of sharp embroidery scissors for cutting threads
Sewing needles for basting and other hand stitching
Cotton sewing threads

Right: Here is the key equipment, aside from a a tape measure and sewing machine, needed for the simplest patchworks. Although the seam marker is a handy optional extra, the rest of the items are essential, so make sure you have them at hand before starting a project.

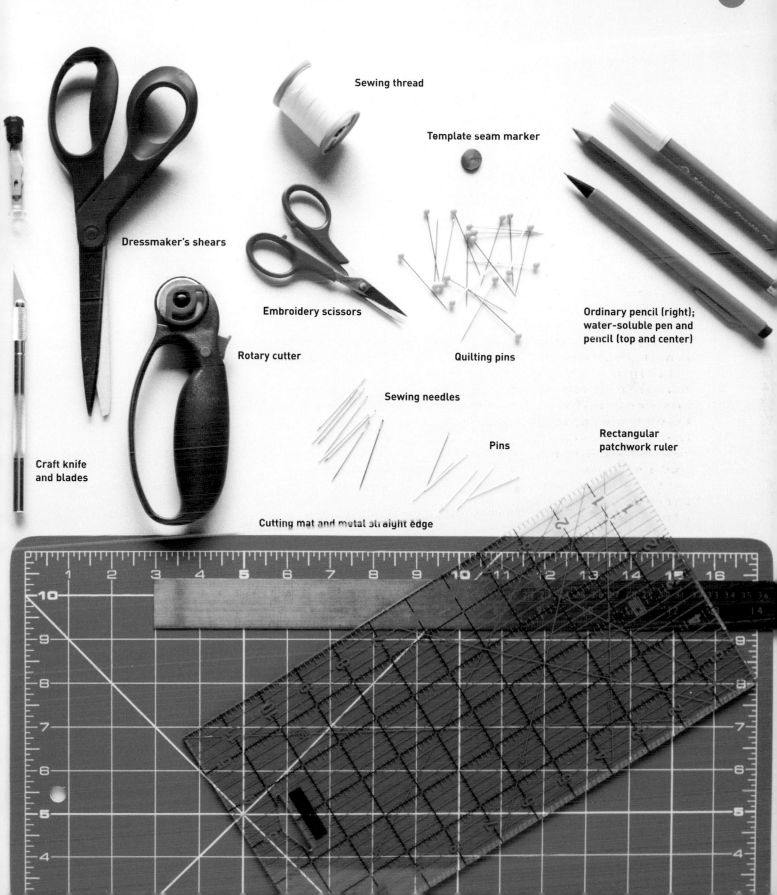

Sewing thread

Template seam marker

Dressmaker's shears

Embroidery scissors

Rotary cutter

Quilting pins

Ordinary pencil (right);
water-soluble pen and
pencil (top and center)

Sewing needles

Pins

Rectangular
patchwork ruler

Craft knife
and blades

Cutting mat and metal straight edge

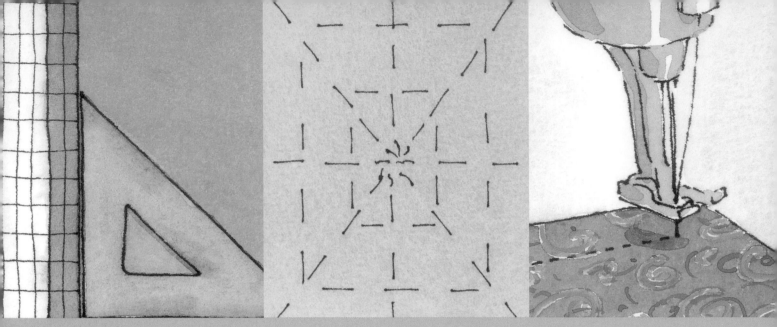

basic

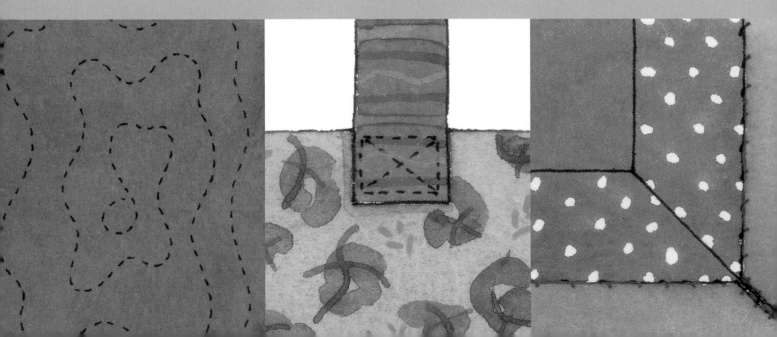

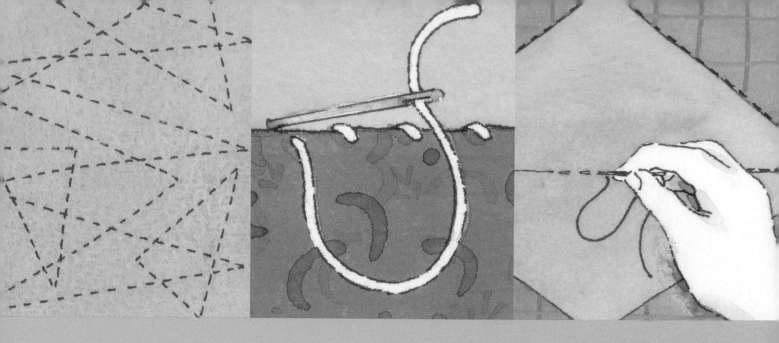

skills

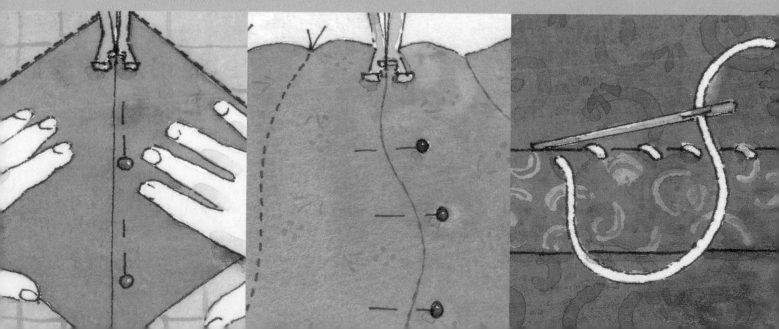

cutting out

Most of the fabric pieces required for the projects in this book are simple squares, rectangles, and strips. These can be cut easily with scissors or a rotary cutter. However, when working with the traditional patchwork patches on pages 56–61, you will need to cut both paper patterns and fabric patches that require special templates.

using patchwork templates

To cut paper and fabric patches for the coaster and mats on pages 56–61, use the actual-size templates on pages 106 and 107. Trace these shapes onto tracing paper or photocopy them, then cut them out. Next, trace the shapes onto stiff, thin cardboard or a sheet of template plastic and cut them out. If you are too impatient to make your own templates, buy them readymade from your local craft store.

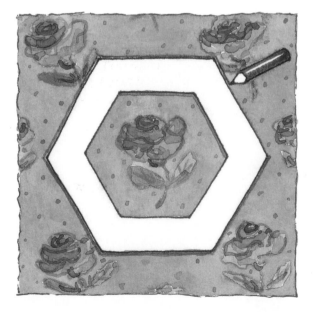

Above: Use a window template if you want to carefully cut a patch from a specific area of a print, for example if you want to frame a flower or motif.

Sometimes it's handy to cut a template with a "window" so that you can position the fabric print exactly within it. Be sure to cut the frame of your window template to the same width as your seam allowance so you can trace the seam line as well (see below left).

cutting patches

When cutting fabric, first check whether the fabric is straight or slightly twisted. A twist, or "bias," in the fabric occurs when the weft lines (the threads running against the selvage) are not precisely perpendicular. This can throw off the accuracy of your work, so it is important to correct it with pressing before you cut your pieces. First, pull out a single weft thread from selvage to selvage; the missing thread will show the path of the the weft threads very clearly. Smooth out the fabric until the weft is perpendicular to the selvages, then press.

Always cut pieces lined up with the straight grain of the fabric (parallel to the selvages or to the weft threads), unless you are cutting bias strips for edgings, which are cut at a 45-degree angle to the selvage.

Fabric can be cut with a pair of sharp dressmaker's shears, or with a rotary cutter if you want to speed up the process or cut several patches at once (see page 13).

rotary cutting

The rotary cutter, cutting mat, and plastic rotary-cutter ruler are an impatient patchworker's dream tools. They allow you to cut fabric pieces quickly and accurately. If you don't already own these and think, as I did, that you can work without them, think again because they really will make your life easier.

The rotary cutter looks a bit scary. It comes with a safety lock, and this must be engaged at all times when the cutter is not in use. Always use the rotary cutter on a self-healing cutting mat.

A purpose-made plastic ruler provides the cutting guide for rotary cutting. Both the cutting mat and the ruler have measurement guides to enable you to cut pieces to the perfect size.

A rotary cutter is great for cutting long strips such as bindings (edgings) and border strips. You can also use one for cutting rectangular and square patches and simple triangles, lining up the fabric edges with the straight and angled lines on the plastic ruler. Most rotary cutters are designed so that the blades can be used on either side of the cutter, which is ideal if you are left handed. A small rotary cutter will cut up to six layers of fabric at a time; a larger one cuts up to eight layers.

USING A ROTARY CUTTER

1 First, press the fabric flat using a steam iron to remove any creases. If you are cutting a large piece of fabric, fold it to fit the cutting mat. Lay the fabric on the mat with the fold facing you. If the fabric is too wide for a single fold, fold it concertina style until it fits the mat.

2 To ensure that the cut strips (or squares or rectangles) are straight and even, start by trimming the edge of the fabric to straighten it. Place a plastic rotary-cutter ruler (or a metal straight edge) over the edge of the fabric, overlapping it by about 1/2in (1cm). Make sure that the ruler is at right angles to the fabric edges and the fold(s) so that the cut will run along the straight grain; use a set square if necessary (see below).

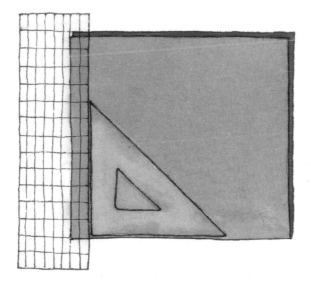

3 Unlock the safety catch on the cutter, press down on the ruler, and wheel the cutter away from you along the edge of the ruler (see below).

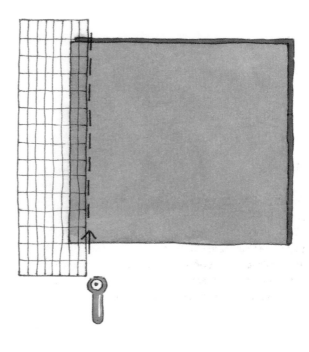

4 You can now cut the first strip of fabric. Several layers of fabric can be cut at once for the strip if required (see below). To cut several layers of square or rectangular patches at once, first cut strips, then lay these on top of each other and cut squares or rectangles off them.

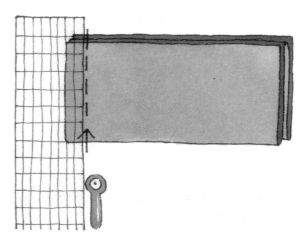

machine and hand stitching

Most of the stitching in this book is done by machine—after all, it is for the impatient patchworker! When using a sewing machine, remember to check that the sewing tension is set correctly for the fabric you are using before you start. Test this on a scrap of fabric. I often forget to do this and then have to rip out stitching, which I hate to do. On the subject of avoiding undoing seams, also always double-check that you are stitching the right pieces together with the correct sides of the fabric facing each other; it is so easy to make mistakes.

A ¼in (6mm) seam allowance is suitable for small patches, and a ½in (1.5cm) seam allowance is fine for larger square or rectangular patches and simple hems.

For items that are going to be washed regularly, it is a good idea to finish the raw edges. I often use the old-fashioned method of pinking edges with a pair of pinking shears, but a machine-zigzagged edge is sturdier. Remember to press seams open as you go.

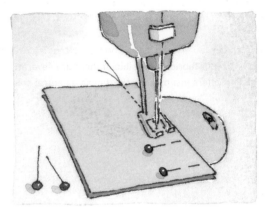

machine stitching

1 Before machine stitching, pin the fabric pieces to each other with the right sides together and the edges aligned. (If there are more than two layers of fabric or the fabric pieces need more stability, baste them together with long running stitches and remove the pins before stitching.)

2 With the machine set at 10–12 stitches to 1in (2.5cm), machine stitch with the pins at right angles to the seam line, removing the pins as you stitch (see top right).

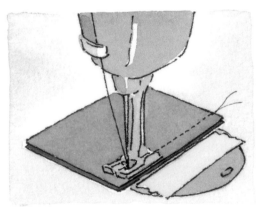

3 In stitching, as in cutting patchwork, it is essential to keep seams even as you are stitching from edge to edge of the fabric pieces. Leave a ¼in (6mm) or ½in (1.5cm) seam allowance as instructed. Follow the seam guide on the machine, or place masking tape on the needle plate at the correct distance from the needle and follow this (see middle right).

4 When stitching around a corner, keep the needle down at the corner point and pivot the fabric (see bottom right).

hand stitching

I have only used a few hand stitches in this book. Although hand sewing sounds laborious and daunting, once you have mastered the stitches, it is quite therapeutic. It is important to produce even, neat stitches, so take the time to practice them first.

Use a good-quality cotton sewing thread that is as near to the color of your fabric as possible. If there are several contrasting colors in a patchwork, choose a neutral color that will blend in easily with the various fabric hues.

Before you start hand stitching, make a knot at the end of the thread. At the end of the seam or hem, secure the thread with a few small stitches in the same place before snipping off the surplus.

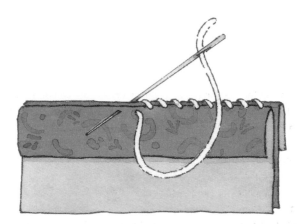

Overcast stitch (also called oversewing)

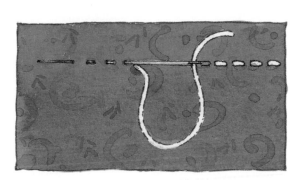

Running stitch

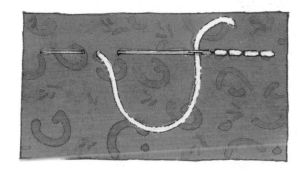

Backstitch

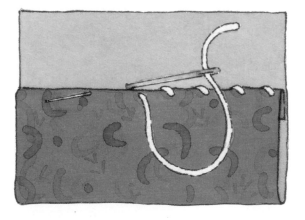

Slip stitch

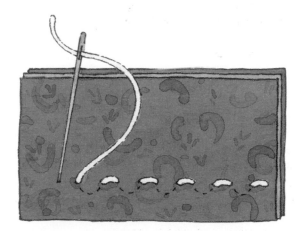

Stab stitch

finishing touches

Here are tips for some of the finishing touches used for the projects in this book, including how to bind (or cover) the raw edges around a patchwork and how to make fabric tubes for hanging loops, bag handles, and ties.

It adds a little time to a project to bind the raw edges with strips of fabric, but it provides a neat, professional-looking finish. Narrow binding is easiest to do with bias-cut strips of fabric, as I did for the place mats on pages 38–41. Bias-cut strips are also used to make piped edgings (see the striped cushions on page 73).

Wide binding is best made either with strips of fabric cut on the straight-grain of the fabric or with the backing fabric or lining folded over onto the front of the patchwork as shown on page 21.

bias binding

To add a simple bias binding to a patchwork project, you first need to cut long strips of fabric on the bias (at a 45-degree angle to the straight grain of the fabric). Strips cut at this angle are stretchy, which allows them to bend neatly around corners.

PREPARING BIAS STRIPS

1 Fold a large square of fabric in half diagonally so that the side and top of the fabric line up together, then cut along the fold (see below).

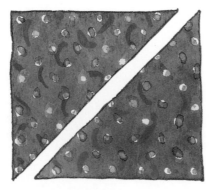

2 With the right sides together, align two straight-grain edges of the pieces and stitch them together with a ¼in (6mm) seam allowance (see below).

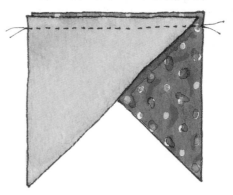

3 Press the seam open, then draw lines across the fabric with a water-soluble pencil, making them parallel to the bias edges and to the desired width of your binding (see below). Cut the strips.

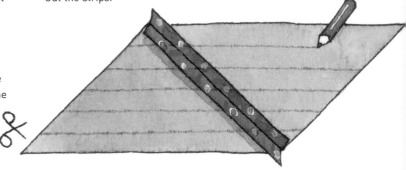

4 Join these strips together end to end into one continuous strip long enough to fit around the entire edge of the item you are binding. Press the seams open (see step 1 on page 73).

5 If you want to use the bias strip for a simple, narrow binding, follow the instructions in step 4 on page 41. To use it for piping, follow the instructions on page 73.

binding with mitered corners

The following instructions are for a self-bound edging with mitered corners—miters are seams stitched in corners at a 45-degree angle. For this edging, the backing fabric is folded over onto the right side of the patchwork top to bind the edge, but you can adapt the principle by turning the top fabric to the wrong side over the backing if you prefer.

When cutting the backing fabric, make sure that it is wider than the patchwork top and the batting. Allow for the finished width of the binding, plus extra for the turn-under. It is easiest to allow for more than you need and then trim the backing to the correct width right before starting the binding. Ensure that the width of the binding is in keeping with the scale of the project. For a large tablecloth, allow at least a 1in (2.5cm) binding and add ¼in (6mm) extra for turning under along the raw edges.

If you are quilting a patchwork, be sure to do this before stitching the binding in place.

STITCHING A MITERED BINDING

1 Trim the lining to the required width of the finished binding plus a turn-under allowance. Clip off the corner of the trimmed border fabric so that it will not poke out past the binding when folded over.

2 Fold each corner point over to the right side of the patchwork top.

3 Fold under ¼in (6mm) along the raw edges and pin in place along one side.

4 Continue pinning arround the edge, carefully matching the folded edges at the corners.

5 Slip stitch the binding in place along the fold line.

6 Slip stitch the mitered corners where the angled edges meet.

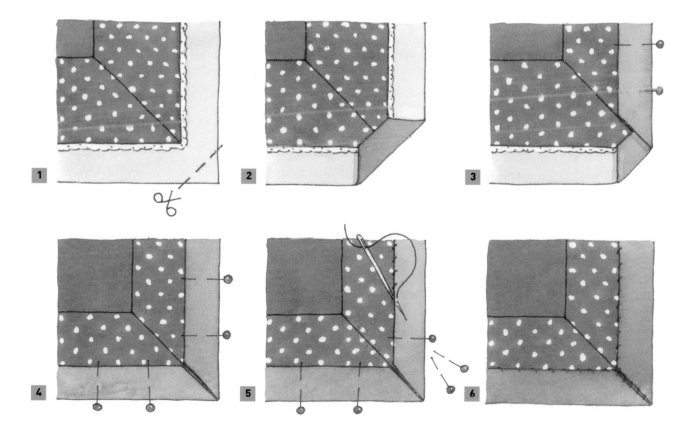

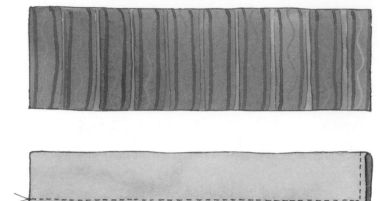

fabric tubes

A few projects in this book use tubes of fabric, either for loops or handles (see the potholders on pages 46–51 and the bags on pages 74–77 and 88–93). The width and length of the tube varies according to the project.

1 To start, cut the fabric to twice the desired finished width of the tube, plus seam allowances, and to the right length, plus seam allowances (see top left). The project instructions provide the precise strip measurements required.

2 Fold the fabric strip in half lengthwise with right sides together and press. Pin the layers together and machine stitch around the edge (see center left).

3 Turn the tube right side out (see bottom left). To do this, either attach a safety pin to one end and use it to draw the fabric through, or poke the end through with the blunt end of a knitting needle. Press flat, aligning the seam with one edge. Turn under the raw edge at the end, press, and stitch.

bag handles

If you are adding handles to a simple patched bag, make the tubes of fabric as shown above to the appropriate width and length. Remember that they will need to be wide enough and strong enough to support heavy weight, and therefore need to be stitched firmly to the bag fabric (ideally, padded to provide support for the stitching).

Sew the handles securely in place by first stitching a square and then stitching across the square diagonally in both directions. Complete as instructed in the relevant project.

quilting

Quilting is a technique so often married to patchwork that it would seem rude to ignore it, even though I have chosen not to quilt most of the projects in this book. Some of my designs have been padded, however, and would look wonderful if they were quilted. Another reason for including this topic is that you may want to expand on the ideas in the book and make your own quilts from some of the piecing ideas I have included.

If you bought this book because you truly are impatient and need quick results, I can't imagine for one moment you would want to hand quilt your projects. The alternative is machine quilting, which is quick and can produce interesting results. On small items, though, it may be easier and more decorative to quilt using a few running stitches.

Whatever kind of quilting you choose, you need to make sure that all the layers to be quilted are firmly held in position. There are several ways to do this; my favourite is to use temporary spray fabric adhesive, which is quick and easy.

Above and left: These details are from the quilted bag (see page 93) in which the bag fabric, the batting, and the lining have been sandwiched together with machine quilting. The petals of the flower fabric provide the guide for the curved quilting (see above), and the straight parallel quilting lines across the top of the bag echo the striped border fabric.

However, the traditional method for securing the layers together prior to quilting is to use basting stitches (long running stitches). Always begin the basting from the middle and smooth out the fabric toward the corners as you go.

Bear in mind that quilting has to be done at the appropriate stage during the stitching of a patchwork and not as an afterthought when the item is finished.

For hand quilting, use a strong quilting thread and a quilting needle. Remember that in some cases stitches will be seen on the other side, so keep them even.

When machine quilting, use a medium-length stitch and a quilting foot on your machine for straight stitching. If you prefer to do free-motion quilting, use a darning or embroidery foot (see opposite page).

Of course, you can expand many of the designs in this book to make wonderful quilts. Just stitch groups of large patches together to form large squares or rectangles, called patchwork blocks, and join these for the quilt center. Then add wide borders to complete the composition.

preparing to quilt

If you want to quilt one of the padded projects in this book, you will need to prepare it properly first. Buy a thin cotton batting for the padding. Before quilting the patchwork top, batting, and backing together, the layers must be firmly secured so they will not shift during the stitching. On projects with a small surface area, you need only baste the layers with a few lines of stitching (see below left), but on larger projects, for example if you make a quilt as an alternative, you must cover the entire surface area with basting to hold the layers together more firmly (see below).

If you do not want to baste the layers together, you can use safety pins instead, inserting them along the diagonal, horizontal, and vertical lines, at suitably spaced intervals.

For very small projects such as the lavender bags on pages 78–83, a button or a strong thread can be used to tie the layers together and provide an attractive finishing detail.

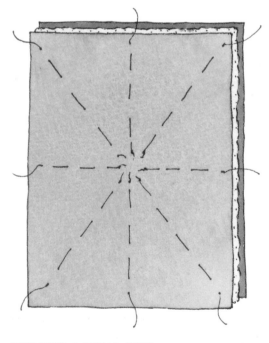

QUILTING A SMALL ITEM
Before quilting a small item, baste the layers of fabric and batting together to secure them, stitching two diagonals and two straight lines as shown.

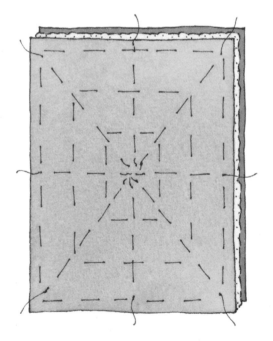

QUILTING A LARGE ITEM
Prepare the layers following the same principle as for a small project, but baste concentric squares as well to fully secure the layers together.

machine quilting

You can quilt in straight lines, straight, or curved geometric patterns, or using an all-over random pattern, known as free-style or free-motion quilting (see right).

For straight lines, use the walking or quilting foot on the machine. The easiest option is to stitch along the seam lines, which provide readymade stitching guides—this is known as quilting or stitching in-the-ditch. Always stitch any straight-line quilting first followed by curved quilting if you are using both techniques in one project.

When quilting a continuous free-style pattern of stitching, be sure to use a longer stitch length than usual to prevent the patchwork from becoming too stiff.

Another good quilting design idea is to follow shapes on the fabric (see page 93), for example the flowers on a floral print or the motifs on a geometric print. Alternatively, you can simply make the quilting up as you go along, in one continuous line of stitching (see right).

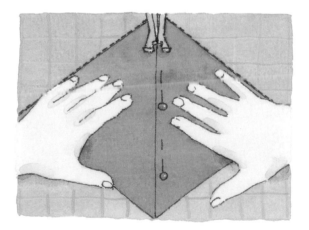

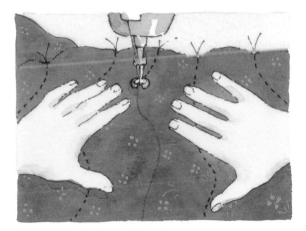

QUILTING STRAIGHT LINES

Always machine quilt in the same direction to prevent the layers from shifting. When stitching long lines, pin the layers together directly on top of the stitching line, removing the pins as you go. To quilt along the seam line (in-the-ditch), follow the seams carefully, using your hands to smooth out and flatten the layers (see above).

FREE-MOTION QUILTING

Use a darning foot and drop the feed dogs to enable you to stitch swifly and evenly over the patchwork surface. Ensure that you are holding the layers securely with your hands, providing a similar tension to that of the machine. This is so that you can control the stitch length and path by evenly moving and swiveling the fabric yourself (see above).

project

gallery

patched and padded hanger

Although covering a hanger hardly sounds like a job for an impatient patchworker, this project makes a unique and attractive small gift, and it is actually very quick and simple to stitch. Once you've made one, you'll be ready to make a whole set because the next few will be much quicker. It's the perfect way to use up scraps, and padded hangers are great for knits or fine silk garments since they prevent fabrics from bulging or snagging.

The color combinations for the patchwork hanger work best with fabrics in strong shades, using one boldly patterned print for the central patch. The key is to ensure that there is continuity in color and tone, but with enough variety to create contrast. Select the floral fabric for the center patch first, then choose harmonizing or contrasting colors for the side patches.

The hangers shown here use Rowan fabrics, but you can create similar ones from your own scraps, if you prefer. Why not make a couple of small hangers for children, using their outgrown dresses or shirts, or stitch a hanger for a special occasion from a discarded evening dress or blouse?

how to make the patched hanger

A traditional wooden hanger forms the base for this project. The one I used measured 16in (40cm) long and 1¼in (3cm) wide, but the cover can be made to fit the proportions of any size hanger. Buy inexpensive wooden hangers in a pack or recycle old ones.

The design shown here uses the Rowan fabrics listed below. The piecing was machine stitched, but you could easily sew the entire patchwork by hand. Make the patches any width, but match the patch widths on both sides of the center patch for symmetry.

The three alternative hangers shown on the opposite page are made with different combinations of fabrics and varying patch widths. You can experiment with your own designs to create a matching set of hangers in different shades of the same print, or use different prints and colorways for each hanger.

materials

For a finished patched and padded hanger measuring approximately ⅝in (1.5cm) longer and wider than your chosen hanger, you will need:
Flat-sided wooden hanger of desired size
Small amount of each of four cotton fabrics as follows—
   A = large-scale floral (ROWAN *Flower Lattice* GP11J)
   B = solid color (ROWAN *Shot Cotton* SC43)
   C = large-scale dot print (ROWAN *Double Ikat Polka* DIP06 Navy)
   D = second solid color (ROWAN *Shot Cotton* SC39)
Cotton batting, at least 1in (2.5cm) longer and wider than length of hanger by twice its width
Matching thread

padding and covering the hanger

1 Cut a strip of batting long enough and wide enough to wrap snuggly around the hanger with the edges fitting together neatly edge to edge. Wrap the batting around the base of the hanger and overcast stitch it in place (see below).

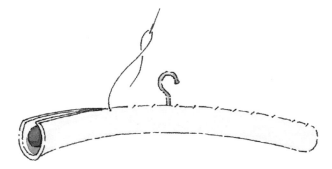

2 Next, measure the length and circumference of the padded hanger to determine the size of the pieced patchwork needed for the cover. Be sure to allow at least an extra ½in (1.5cm) all around the outside edge of the patchwork.

3 Allowing ½in (1.5cm) for the seam allowances between the patches, cut the fabric patches for the sleeve (see below)— one patch from fabric A and two each from fabrics B, C, and D. Pin and machine stitch the patches to each other, with right sides together and working from the center outward as shown by the arrows. Press the seams open.

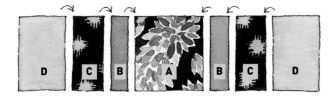

4 Fold the patchwork in half lengthwise with right sides together and press. Baste the raw edges together at each end to fit the hanger. Before turning the patchwork right side out, slip it onto the hanger to check the fit. Adjust the positions of the seams if necessary. Machine stitch and remove the basting (see below). Trim these end seams to ½in (1.5cm).

5 Turn the patchwork right side out, and slip it back onto the hanger. Turn under the raw edges along the top and hand sew in place (see below), using stab stitch (see page 19).

mixed-print cushion

There are no strictly set patch sizes for this cushion design—you can just sew rectangular and square patches together in any combination you like. Feel free to play around with the piecing method shown on the following pages, as long as you keep in mind that your square and rectangular patches need to fit together to form bigger squares and rectangles. If you wish, you could make a big quilt using the same technique and joining big patched squares like this together in rows.

I chose cotton fabrics within a specific color range to create two different versions of the cushion. When mixing prints—in this case florals and geometrics—ensure that you keep the color strengths (known technically as saturation or depth of color) similar. This will help pull very dissimilar prints together and give an exciting spontaneous look to the cushion.

I did not design the two different colorways of this cushion to go together, but they actually looked surprisingly good as a combination. Half the fun of patchwork comes from the surprises you get while designing and making!

how to make the mixed-print cushion

This square patchwork cushion has a simple "envelope" back that consists of two pieces of overlapping fabric. The width of the overlap should be no less than 5in (12cm), as narrower overlaps will gape open.

The cushion shown here and on the previous page is made up of toning oranges, ochers, and greens in Rowan fabrics that include a floral, a dot print, two stripes, and a solid. An alternative colorway, made with the same method but in mauves and pinks, is shown on pages 36 and 37.

Although my cushion measures 16in (40cm) square when finished, you could easily enlarge or reduce the finished size by cutting bigger or smaller patches. But remember that it is easiest to make a cushion cover to a size that will fit a standard-size pillow form.

materials

For a finished cushion measuring 16in (40cm) square, you will need:
Small amount of each of the following five cotton fabrics—
 A = dot print (ROWAN *Dotty* GP140),
 B = wide stripe (ROWAN *Broad Stripe* BS11)
 C = random stripe (ROWAN *Exotic Stripe* ES20)
 D = solid color (ROWAN *Shot Cotton* SC35)
 E = large-scale floral (ROWAN *Floral Dance* GP120)
45cm (1/2yd) of 44in (112cm) wide cotton fabric of your choice (**F**), for cushion back
Matching thread
Pillow form, 16in (40cm) square

making the patchwork

1 For the cushion front, cut out the five patches that include 1/2in (1.5cm) seam allowances. Cut one patch 12in by 9in (31cm by 23cm) from fabric A, one patch each 6in by 9in (15cm by 23cm) from fabrics B and C, one patch 5in by 9in (13cm by 23cm) from fabric D, and one patch 8in by 9in (21cm by 23cm) from fabric E. Pay attention to the direction of the stripes when cutting the stripe fabrics (see below).

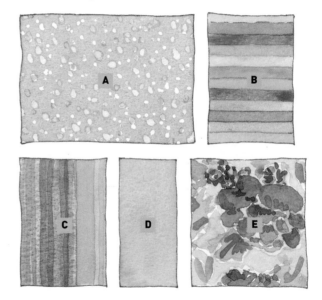

2 With right sides together, pin fabric A to fabric B and machine stitch (see below). Press the seams open.

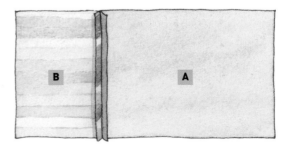

3 Sew together fabrics C, D, and E in the same way (see below). Press the seams open.

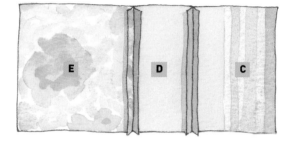

4 To complete the pieced cushion front, sew together the two sections just made, pinning, machine stitching, and pressing as before.

sewing on the back

1 For the cushion cover back, cut out two rectangles, each 17in by 11½in (43cm by 29cm), from fabric F.

2 Turn under ½in (1.5cm) along one long edge of each rectangle to form a hem and press. Pin each hem in position and machine stitch. Overlap the two back pieces by 5in (12cm) so that they form a single piece the same size as the cushion front (see below), and pin them together.

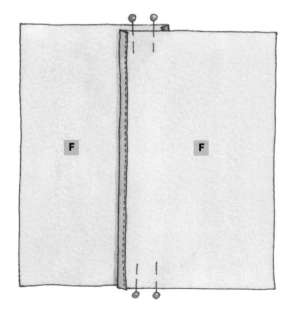

3 Pin and baste the cushion back pieces to the pieced cushion front, with the right sides together. Machine stitch and remove the basting (see below).

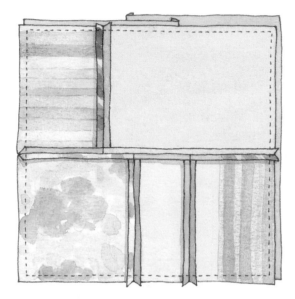

4 To ensure crisp corners, clip off a triangle of the seam allowances at each of the four corners of the cover before turning it right side out. To do this, cut diagonally across the corner about ⅛in (3mm) from the seam. Turn the cushion cover right side out and insert the pillow form.

alternative colorway

You can make the same style cushion in alternative colorways using the fabrics of your choice and cutting different rectangular patch shapes. For the cushion shown on the right, I used predominantly striped and plain fabrics. These mixed-print cushions are very quick to put together, so why not make a stylish set of three or four in different colorways?

The piecing pattern below would also make a great quilt or throw. To do this, simply sew together similar large squares, rotating them at random. Then complete the patchwork with a wide border.

Choose five cotton fabrics from your scrap collection for this cushion (see below)—two different stripes (**A** and **B**), two solid colors (**C** and **E**), and a dot print (**D**). Alternatively, buy the Rowan fabrics used here—*Exotic Stripe* ES10 (**A**), *Rowan Stripe* RS04 (**B**), *Shot Cotton* SC17 (**C**), *Dotty* GP14T (**D**), and *Shot Cotton* SC07 (**E**).

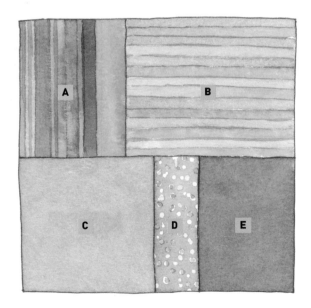

striped
place mat

Padded place mats are excellent if you love to serve dinner on warm plates because the batting provides the necessary insulation for protecting your table. I chose a design that looks ideal with a contemporary place setting in which all the cutlery is set at one end; the striped panel separates the cutlery from the plate. But, of course, you can use them however you wish.

If you prefer a flatter, neater finish for the mats, you can quilt them very easily in a simple striped design, as shown on page 41. Full instructions for quilting are given on pages 23–25.

For matching napkins, follow the basic place mat design, but cut the main fabric into a 12in (30cm) square for each napkin. Then use either the floral binding fabric or the striped fabric to make a single off-center stripe down one side of each napkin.

how to make the striped place mat

This place mat is very simple to make: the patchwork consists of just three pieces of fabric—two in the same plain fabric and one in a contrasting stripe. Sewing on the simple binding in a contrasting fabric is a bit more time consuming, but even making a set of six tablemats will not take very long at all.

If you want, back the place mat with a contrasting fabric so it is reversible, follow the instructions on page 21. In this binding method, excess backing fabric is folded around to the front to form a neat contrasting edging.

I have included a quilted alternative to the mat (see opposite page). It has a flatter finish, but you will have to be prepared to spend a bit more time on this version.

The place mat shown here measures 14in by 10in (36cm by 25cm), but you can adjust it to any size by cutting the pieces in step 1 to the desired size of the finished place mat and cutting the stripe insert in step 2 long enough to fit the width of the finished place mat.

materials

For two finished place mats each measuring 14in by 10in (36cm by 25cm), you will need:
Three 112cm (44in) wide cotton fabrics as follows—
  A = 70cm (³/₄yd) of solid color (ROWAN *Shot Cotton* SC31)
  B = small amount of random stripe (ROWAN *Exotic Stripe* ES21)
  C = 45cm (¹/₂yd) of floral print (ROWAN *Chrysanthemum* GP13R), for binding
Cotton batting, same size as finished place mat
Matching thread

cutting and stitching the mat

1 Cut two rectangles from fabric A, each 14in by 10in (36cm by 25cm), for the front and back of the mat. Cut a rectangle of batting to the same size. Then cut the front into two pieces, 3¹/₄in (8.5cm) from the edge (see below).

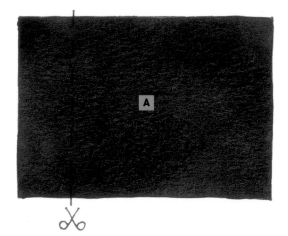

2 Cut a piece of fabric B measuring 10in by 2¹/₄in (25cm by 6cm). Position B between the two pieces of the front. With right sides facing, pin both pieces of A to B and machine stitch, leaving a ¹/₂in (1.5cm) seam allowance. Press the seams open. Trim the front to the same size as the back.

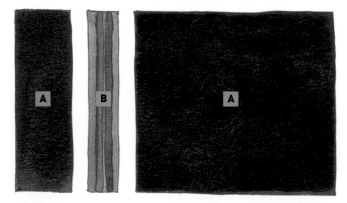

3 Sandwich the batting between the back and the patchwork front. Pin and baste the layers together.

4 Prepare a bias strip of fabric C for the binding, 1¹/₂in (4cm) wide and long enough to fit around the mat (see page 20). Starting at one corner, pin the binding to the front of the mat, aligning the raw edges and leaving a 1in (2.5cm) free end at the start as shown (see below). Baste and machine stitch the binding ³/₈in (1cm) from the edge and join the ends.

5 Remove the basting. Then press the binding away from the center of the front and fold it snugly over to the back of the mat. Turn under ³/₈in (1cm) and pin the folded edge to the back of the mat. Hand sew the binding in place (see below) using slip stitch (see page 19).

alternative design

If you wish, you can quilt the place mat. I chose to stitch simple vertical quilting lines, echoing the line of the striped fabric. The quilting lines are spaced random widths apart, rather than forming a strictly geometric pattern. This method is also much quicker.

Carry out the quilting after you have basted the batting between the front and back of the mat and before you add the binding.

Follow the instructions for machine quilting on pages 23–25. To make sure your quilting lines are straight, you can draw them with tailor's chalk or a water-soluble pen and remove the drawn lines later.

clothespin bag

This clothespin bag is perfect for brightening your washday. It incorporates a small wooden child's clothing hanger, which many clothespin bags relied upon in times gone by. You can usually find these small wooden hangers in department stores, but if you can't, thrift stores sometimes have them. If all else fails, shorten a standard-size wooden hanger to the length you want using a saw.

This time around I have mixed a very bright, splashy print with two strong contrasting colors In plain fabrics, but you could make your own fabric choice—perhaps swapping a toning stripe for one of the plain fabrics, if you wish.

The bag would also serve well hanging on a cupboard door for socks or tights, which otherwise tend to scramble together in a drawer. Just make a bigger version with a grownup-size hanger.

how to make the clothespin bag

The coat hanger determines the shape of this bag. To adapt the bag to fit a different hanger size from the one used here, cut the fabric pieces as wide as your hanger, plus 1½in (5cm) extra to allow for the hanger thickness and the ½in (1.5cm) seams. The bag is machine stitched, but is small enough to hand stitch if you prefer.

materials

For a finished clothespin bag measuring approximately 14in by 12in (35cm by 30cm), you will need:
Wooden coat hanger 11½in (33cm) wide (child's size)
Three 44in (112cm) wide cotton fabrics as follows—
  A = ½yd (45cm) of a large-scale floral (ROWAN *Floral Dance* GP12P)
  B = small amount of a solid color (ROWAN *Shot Cotton* SC41)
  C = ½yd (45cm) of a second solid color (ROWAN *Shot Cotton* SC34)
Matching thread

cutting and stitching the bag

1 Start by cutting out the fabric pieces that include the ½in (1.5cm) seam allowances as follows:
For the top front, cut a piece 13in by 5in (33cm by 13cm) from fabric A, a strip 13in by 2in (33cm by 5.5cm) from fabric B, a strip 13in by 1¾in (33cm by 5cm) from fabric C, and a piece of lining 13in by 6¾in (33cm by 17.5cm) from fabric C.
For the bottom front, cut a piece 13in by 7½in (33cm by 19cm) from fabric A, a strip 13in by 2in (33cm by 5.5cm) from fabric B, a strip 13in by 1¾in (33cm by 5cm) from fabric C, and a piece of lining 13in by 9¼in (33cm by 23.5cm) from fabric C.
For the back, cut a piece 13in by 15in (33cm by 38cm) from fabric A and a piece for the lining of the same size.

2 To make the top of the front of the bag, pin, then machine stitch the front pieces together in the order shown (see below), with right sides together and leaving ½in (1.5cm) seam allowances. Press the seams open, then fold and press the lining behind the pieced patches, with wrong sides together.

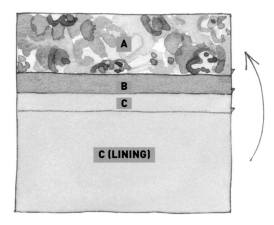

3 Make the bottom front in the same way (see below).

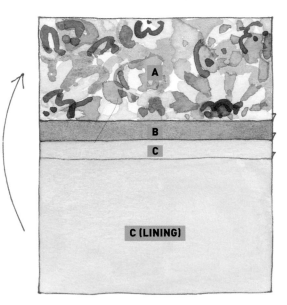

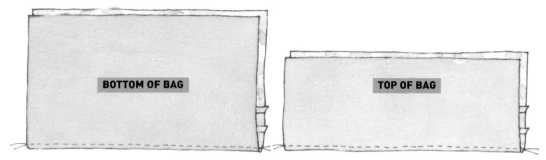

4 Topstitch close to the seam line on the lined bottom and top sections of the bag (see above).

5 Place the floral back of the bag on top of the back lining with the wrong sides together. Then pin the lined top and bottom front pieces to the back and back lining, with the right sides of the front and back together. Place the hanger on the top of the bag, and draw around the top of the hanger with tailor's chalk or a water-soluble pen (see below) so that the line just touches the top edge of the bag.

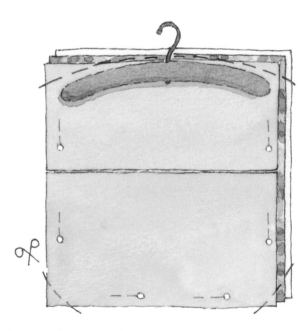

6 Remove the hanger. Starting and finishing at the center (see above), machine stitch around the clothespin bag, leaving a ½in (1.5cm) seam allowance and leaving a gap at the top just large enough for the hanger hook to be pushed through. Finish the raw edges either with a machine zigzag stitch or with pinking shears. Hand sew together each end of the front opening to about 2in (5cm) from the seam line.

7 Turn the bag right side out and insert the hanger.

Draw matching curved lines around the bottom corners of the bag (you can use the edge of a plate as a template), and trim away the curved corners (see above).

potholder

This potholder is based on a variation of traditional log cabin patchwork. Once you realize how simple the technique is, you may find yourself hooked and you'll want to work more traditional log cabin designs (see pages 50 and 51).

I like the idea of taking the log-cabin technique out of its usual context and playing with it a little. Using it for a potholder gives an everyday object a highly individual design and highlights the simple, elegant geometry of the log-cabin block.

The potholder needs fabrics that work well together to produce interesting contrasts and harmonies of color. The original concept of the log-cabin design was that the central square represented the fire in the hearth and the cabin's walls of stacked logs were built around it. On the more traditional log-cabin designs, therefore, the central square is red, and the surrounding strips of fabric are dark on one side and light on the other to depict the shadows of the fire. There is also a theory that the design is based on the conjoining squares and rectangles of communal field layouts. Whichever is true, the technique is actually a lot simpler than it looks, and the design possibilities, both in positioning of color and the layout of the strips, are worth exploring.

how to make the potholder

This log-cabin-style patchwork is made up of two squares and a series of seven surrounding strips, each the length of the previously joined patches. I found it easiest to cut five long strips, then to cut the individual pieces from these strips. Each strip is 2in (5.2cm) wide and includes the seam allowances.

The order of applying all the strips for the potholder shown on page 47 is shown in step 5 on page 49, but if you are making several, be sure to try out the other strip formats shown on pages 50 and 51.

materials

For a finished potholder measuring 7½in (20cm) square, you will need:

Small amount of each of five to nine different cotton
    fabrics in the chosen toning color scheme
Cotton batting, 8½in by 17in (23cm by 46cm)
Matching thread

cutting and stitching the potholder

1 Cut a strip 2in (5.2cm) wide and at least 10in (27cm) long from each of your different fabrics.

2 For patches 1 and 2, cut a 2in (5.2cm) square from two different fabric strips. Pin and machine stitch patch 2 to patch 1, with right sides together and leaving a ¼in (6mm) seam allowance (see below). Press the seam open.

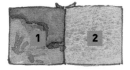

3 For patch 3, pin and machine stitch a third fabric strip to patches 1 and 2, aligning one end of the strip with one end of the joined patches. Then cut off the excess fabric from patch 3 (see below) and press the seam open.

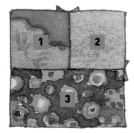

4 Use a fourth fabric strip for patch 4, stitching it to patches 1 and 3 and then trimming off the excess in the same way as before (see below). Press the seam open.

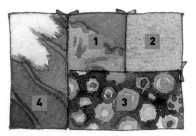

5 Continue adding strips in the same way in the order shown (see above) until all nine patches are joined on. You can use a fabric more than once as long as it is not touching a patch of the same fabric. Cut more strips as they are needed.

6 For the back of the potholder, cut a piece of plain fabric and a double layer of cotton batting, both to the same size as the newly formed patchwork.

7 Next, make the hanging loop for the potholder. Cut a strip 1½in (4.2cm) wide and 5in (13cm) long. Fold the strip in half lengthwise with right sides together and pin. To form a tube, machine stitch along the long side of the strip, ¼in (6mm) from the raw edges. Turn the tube right side out and press. (See page 22 for more about making tubes of fabric.) Fold the hanging loop in half widthwise and baste the ends together about ¼in (6mm) from the raw edges. The ends of the hanging loop will be caught in the potholder seam, so they do not need to be hemmed.

8 Position the layers ready to be stitched in the following order—batting, backing fabric (right side facing upward), hanging loop in one corner with the tails protruding, and finally the patchwork (wrong side facing upward).

9 Pin, baste, then machine stitch, leaving a gap for turning right side out (see below). Snip off the corners and trim off excess batting close to the seam. Turn right side out.

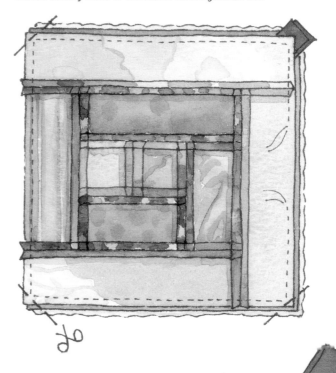

10 Hand sew the opening closed (see below).

alternative potholder designs

Here are two other versions of the log-cabin-style patchwork, one in Rowan fabrics in burnt oranges and ochers, and the other in blues. They are made from an interesting mix of prints and plain fabric. The patches for these variations are pieced in a different way than described in the instructions on pages 48 and 49. The piecing for the potholder on the opposite page is begun with a strip of three squares. For the potholder shown below, the piecing is started with a single square at one corner. Just study the contrasting strips to determine the order in which the remaining patches are added.

check
tablecloth

This tablecloth is incredibly simple to make, yet creates a very striking visual effect. The hand-hemmed edge gives a nice finish, but if you want to be quick, you can machine topstitch the edge instead.

The fabric combination used here invokes a modern country mood, but there are endless possibilities at your disposal. Just choose colors and prints that complement the decor of your home or your china.

Obviously, by adding more squares or taking some away you can easily alter the size of the tablecloth. If you want to go to a bit more trouble, you could add a matching or contrasting border to the cloth or make a set of matching napkins.

This geometric check design would also make a good duvet cover, which can be simply made by creating what is basically a large bag with ties at one end to close it. You could patch the cover all over, as with the tablecloth, or run strips of patches between wide bands of plain fabric. Use an old sheet, dyed, to form the backing. Most duvet covers are too wide for traditional bolts of fabric and the fabrics have to be seamed anyway, so a patchwork duvet sidesteps this problem rather neatly.

how to make the check tablecloth

I cut the check squares for this patchwork one at a time so I could frame a certain area. If you prefer to cut the squares from precut strips of fabric, just substitute the check fabric for a plain one.

materials

For a tablecloth measuring approximately 44½in (111cm) square, you will need:
Two 44in (112cm) wide cotton fabrics as follows—
  A = 1½yd (140cm) of a check (ROWAN *Double Ikat Checkboard* DIC06 Blue)
  B = 1½yd (140cm) of a large-scale floral (ROWAN *Peony* GP17BL)
Matching thread

making the patchwork

1 Cut out twelve 10in (25.5cm) squares from check-fabric A and thirteen 10in (25.5cm) squares from floral-fabric B (see below). When cutting the check fabric, I made sure that the checks were centered on each patch so that I could then use the edges of the checks as guides for my seam lines. To do this, you need to cut each piece individually. Cut the floral patches individually, too, if you want to frame a particular area or motif.

2 If you are using the checks on the check patches as guides for your seam lines, neaten the edges of all the patches with a zigzag stitch or pinking shears. Otherwise, leave the neatening until after each seam is stitched.

3 Starting with a check square, arrange a row of five patches, alternating the check and floral squares. With right sides together, pin and machine stitch these patches to each other, leaving a ½in (1.5cm) seam allowance (see below). Press the seams open.

4 After stitching together the first row of five patches, sew four more rows in the same way, but starting each five-patch row with a different fabric patch. Press the seams open as you go.

5 Pin the completed rows together one at a time, matching the seams exactly by pinning through them (see below). Machine stitch the rows together and press the seams open.

hemming the tablecloth

1 To hem the tablecloth, turn under and press ½in (1.5cm) all around the edge, then turn under ½in (1.5mm) again and pin the hem in place as you press. Baste, then hand stitch the hem (see below), using slip stitch (see page 19). Alternatively, if you are in a hurry, you can turn under ¼in (6mm) twice and topstitch using a sewing machine.

2 Remove the basting and press the finished hem.

napkin alternative

The tablecloth would look great with matching napkins with a contrasting border. Cut a 12in (30cm) square for each napkin. For a 1in (2.5cm) wide contrasting border, cut four 3in (8cm) wide strips. Cut two of the strips 12in (30cm) long and two 13in (33cm) long. Fold under and press ½in (1.5cm) along each long side of each strip. Then press the strips in half lengthwise. Pin and sew the shorter strips in place over opposite edges of the napkin, then sew on the longer strips, turning under the ends. Alternatively, back the napkins and make a mitered edging as shown on page 21.

coasters and mats

The hexagon has always been associated with classic old-fashioned patchwork, and I thought it was important to include this time-honored, interesting technique in the book.

I came across an inexpensive bag of half-finished patchwork in a thrift store and bought it because I thought it might be inspirational—and because I can never resist a bargain. As it turned out, the bag contained templates, cut and hemmed fabric hexagons, and an abundance of ready-cut paper hexagons. This was an unexpected gift, the head start that I needed, and I was soon deciding on my own fabric combinations and sewing together the patches. I found myself hooked, always telling myself I'd stop after "just one more patch."

The hexagon coasters and the star mat that follow are excellent starter projects if you have always been intrigued by such traditional patchwork techniques, but have been too daunted to try them. After they start working their magic on you, you may find yourself starting a quilt using one of these great little shapes.

how to make the hexagonal coaster

Use the instructions that follow to make the coasters shown below and on page 56. The coasters are backed with felt, which is sturdy and doesn't fray.

You could, of course, use a larger patch size to make a circular tablecloth, for example, or to make a throw entirely from hexagons.

materials

For a finished coaster measuring approximately 6in (15cm) in diameter, you will need:
Small amount of each of six different cotton prints and one solid color (ROWAN *Shot Cotton*), in your chosen toning color scheme
Felt for backing coaster
Matching thread

making the patchwork

1 Trace the hexagon templates (see page 106) and carefully transfer them onto stiff, thin cardboard (see below).

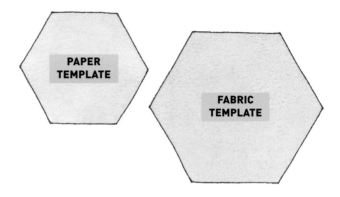

PAPER TEMPLATE

FABRIC TEMPLATE

2 Using the smaller template, trace the required number of hexagons onto paper and cut these out—you will need seven papers per coaster. Using the larger template, cut out a corresponding number of fabric hexagons, one from each fabric. If you want to position a print very precisely, use a window template (see page 16).

3 Place a paper pattern in the center of the wrong side of your first fabric hexagon. Fold the seam allowance over the paper and baste through both layers of fabric and the paper (see below). Repeat for the other patches.

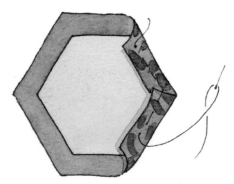

4 With right sides together, overcast stitch the central patch (the solid-colored one) to one of the other patches, stitching along one side of the hexagons (see below). Take care to avoid the paper patterns inside. (It is not a disaster if you catch the paper once or twice as you stitch, but it will rip the paper template when you remove it.)

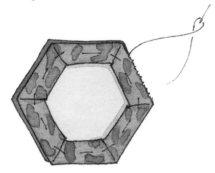

5 Sew the next patch to the first two (see below). Sew on the remaining hexagons to complete the patchwork, then press. You can remove the central hexagon paper at this stage, but leave the others in place.

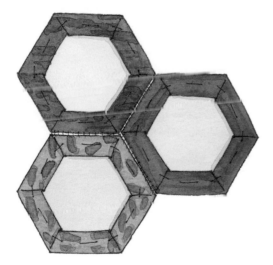

backing the coaster

1 Place your finished patchwork on the felt and, using tailor's chalk or water-soluble pen, draw around the edge. Remove the patchwork and cut out the felt back (see below).

2 With wrong sides together, overcast stitch the felt to the patched coaster (see below). Take out each paper pattern as you complete the stitching around each hexagon except for the final patch—you will have to carefully remove the last paper before stitching or it will be trapped in the coaster forever. Finally, press with a steam iron.

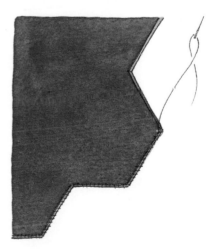

how to make the star-patchwork mat

The small mat on the opposite page is a variation on the hexagon coaster, but it uses diamond and triangle templates instead, to form a star pattern. Take special care when sewing the diamonds at the center point.

materials

For a finished mat measuring approximately 8½in (21.5cm) in diameter, you will need:
Small amount of each of three cotton fabrics as follows—
A = solid color [ROWAN *Shot Cotton* SC10]
B = medium-scale floral [ROWAN *Flower Sprays* LC01BK]
C = second solid color [ROWAN *Shot Cotton* SC01]
Felt for backing mat
Matching thread

making the patchwork

1 Trace the diamond and triangle templates (pages 106 and 107) and carefully transfer them onto stiff, thin cardboard.

2 Using the smaller templates, trace eight diamonds and eight triangles onto paper and cut these out. Using the larger templates, cut out four fabric diamonds each from fabrics A and B, and eight fabric triangles from fabric C.

3 Place a paper pattern in the center of the wrong side of each fabric patch (see below). Fold the seam allowance

over the paper and pin it in place. At the points, carefully pinch the seam allowance together out of the way, or fold it neatly as shown. Baste the seam allowance in place, stitching through the paper and both layers of fabric.

4 With right sides together, overcast stitch a fabric-A diamond patch (a solid-colored patch) to a fabric-B diamond patch (a floral-print patch), stitching along one side of the diamonds as shown (see below).

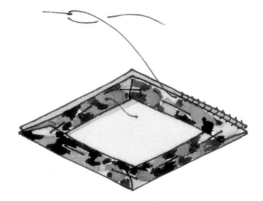

5 Sew all the diamonds together in pairs as for the first pair, then sew them into groups of four, alternating fabric-A and fabric-B patches. Finally, stitch the two halves of the star together, being careful to stitch across the joins so that the points all meet neatly at the center.

6 Join each triangle to each pair of stars and press carefully.

7 Finally, back the star patchwork with felt as for the coaster on page 59.

a p r o n

I am not sure whether this apron can technically be described as patchwork, but it is made from more than one fabric, and I like the idea of using a print for the borders. If you want to give it a more patchworked look, then use the border fabric for the pockets, too.

The pleated sides give it an attractively feminine shape, and the extra width in the apron means that you don't get floury hand-marks on your clothes (something I find only too easy to do when cooking in a traditional smaller apron).

This pattern gets its inspiration from a vintage apron that I wear often because it is both comfortable and flattering. I borrowed the ideas of the stripes from a traditional chef's apron.

how to make the apron

This apron is quite easy to make. The double hems around the skirt are simply folded under and topstitched in place.

The binding around the neck joins a simple double pleat in the waist ties at the side, making the apron roomy and comfortable to wear.

materials

For a finished apron measuring 34in (87cm) long from the top of the bib by 32in (80cm) wide, you will need:
Two 44in (112cm) wide Rowan cottons as follows—
A = 1yd (90cm) of a wide stripe (ROWAN *Broad Stripe* BS11)
B = 1/2yd (45cm) of a small-scale circular print (ROWAN *Paperweight* GP20PN)
Matching thread

cutting and stitching the apron

1 From striped-fabric A, cut out the main body of the apron (see below), so that the skirt measures 33in (83cm) wide by 26 1/2in (65.5cm) tall and the bib measures 10in (25cm) wide by 8in (23cm) tall (see page 106 for the pattern-piece diagram). Make sure the stripes are running vertically (see below).

2 For the pockets, cut two rectangles, each 10in (26cm) wide by 7 1/2in (19.5cm) long, from fabric A. Cut them so that the stripes run horizontally (see top left on bottom of page 64).

3 Fold under and press 1/2in (1.5cm) along the sides and bottom edges of the apron (see below). Then fold under 1/2in (1.5cm) again and pin, mitering the corners as shown (see bottom left). Topstitch close to the first fold and press.

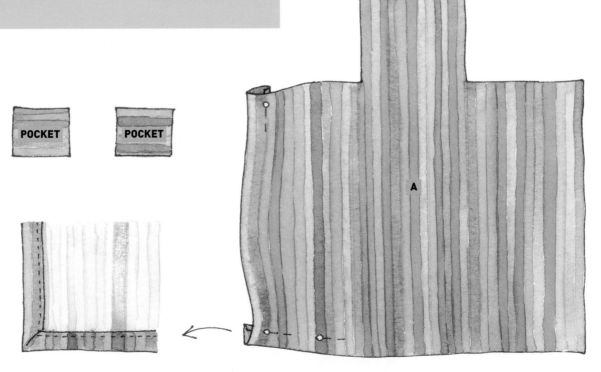

POCKET POCKET

A

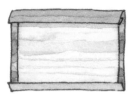

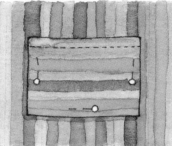

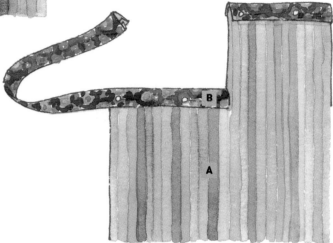

4 Turn under and press ½in (1.5cm) along the side and bottom edges of each pocket. Then turn under and press a neat ½in (1.5cm) double hem along the top edge as for the apron hems (see above left). Topstitch the double hem close to the first fold. Pin and baste the pockets to your apron in the desired positions (see above right and page 62). Topstitch along the sides and bottom of each pocket to secure. Remove the basting and press.

sewing on the binding

1 For the binding, cut 3in (8cm) wide strips from fabric B. Cut two 35in (91cm) strips for the waist ties, one 10in (25cm) strip for the top edge of the bib, and one 42in (105cm) strip for the neck loop and bib side-edges.

2 Fold under and press ½in (1.5cm) along each long edge of each binding strip. Then fold each strip in half lengthwise with right sides together and press again.

3 Pin and baste one end of the waist-tie bindings over the waistline edges of the apron, and pin and baste the remaining length of binding together to form the ties, turning under the ends. Pin and baste the shortest piece of binding to the top of the bib (see top right). Topstitch these bindings.

4 Fold under and press ½in (1.5cm) at each end of the neck binding before positioning it. Pin the neck binding to the bib as shown, catching in a double 1in (2.5cm) pleat in the waistline binding at each end (see right). Try on the apron and adjust the length of the neck binding to fit. Baste and topstitch the binding. Then, stitch a square over the pleat to secure. Remove the basting and press.

striped
runner

Striped patchworks are great for creating a whole range of household textiles, from duvet covers and table runners to chair or sofa throws. They can be very simple or much more complex, depending on the number of strips, or stripes, you use.

The impact of the design is produced by the combination of colors and print patterns you choose, so you need to think quite carefully about the setting in which you use such graphic pieces. They look great in bold colors in an otherwise minimal setting, perhaps bringing to life a plain monochromatic room or showing off a set of plain white china. If you want a more "boho" look, you can use narrower stripes in toning colors that will mix and match with other patterned fabrics in the space.

You could very easily add more stripes to make a picnic blanket, for example, in which case it would be a good idea to back the fabric with a contrasting lining that could be used to create a self-edging on the front (see page 21).

how to make the striped runner

This striped runner is the most basic patchwork project in this book, but you must be careful to cut the stripes precisely on the straight grain of the fabric, as any deviation will show up on a larger item.

This particular runner measures 22½in (59cm) wide and can be made to any length you like. If you make the runner longer than 42in (105cm), you will not be able to cut the pieces across the width of the fabric and will need to buy lengths of fabric that are the length of your runner, plus seam allowances. You can use the surplus fabric for the backing and to make other small projects.

Another way to use your fabric economically is to patch the stripes with long rectangles of different matching colors. For an inexpensive backing, try using an old sheet dyed to match in the washing machine.

I have also included a suggestion for a variation that would make a great throw (see opposite page).

materials

For a finished runner measuring 22½in (59cm) wide by by up to 42in (105cm) long (see above for fabric amounts for a longer runner), you will need:
Three 44in (112cm) wide cotton fabrics as follows—
  A = ¼yd (25cm) of a large-scale floral (ROWAN *Damask* GP02J)
  B = ½yd (45cm) of a solid color (ROWAN *Shot Cotton* SC22)
  C = 1yd (90cm) of a second solid color (ROWAN *Shot Cotton* SC33)
Matching thread

making the patchwork

1 First cut out the patch strips (see below). Cut all the strips the same length—the desired length of your finished runner plus a ½in (1.5cm) seam allowance at each end. From fabric A, cut one strip 8½in (22cm) wide. From fabric B, cut two strips each 5½in (15cm) wide. From fabric C, cut two strips each 4in (11cm) wide.

2 Arrange the strips with the floral fabric in the center as shown (see above). Pin and machine stitch the panels to each other, with the right sides together and leaving ½in (1.5cm) seam allowances. Press the seams open.

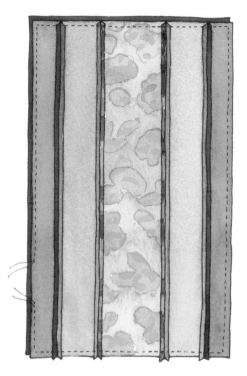

backing the runner

1 Cut a piece of backing from fabric C to the same size as the finished patchwork.

2 Place the patched front on top of the lining, right sides together. Pin together all around the edges. Machine stitch, leaving a ½in (1.5cm) seam allowance and leaving a small opening at one side (see left).

3 To ensure crisp corners, clip off a triangle of the seam allowance at each of the four corners. To do this, cut diagonally across the corner about ⅛in (3mm) from the seam. Pull the runner through the opening in the stitching to turn it right side out. Press carefully, turning under the raw edges at the opening.

4 Finally, topstitch all around the edges of the runner, closing the opening as you do so.

alternative design

You could vary the basic runner design to create a throw or quilt by cutting wider strips and adding striped borders across the top and bottom (see right). If you pad a large design, be sure to quilt it to keep the batting in place (see pages 23–25).

Alternatively, you could make a version with narrower strips repeated more frequently across the runner, or you could ring the changes by patching the center panel from six large rectangles, using a different floral fabric for each.

striped cushions

These two cushions are fun to make because they play with stripe formations, using only one fabric for the main patchwork plus a contrasting piped edging cut from a print with a pattern of circles. They take a little more thought and effort than other projects in this book, but they offer a good introduction to some of the concepts of traditional patchwork if you find that you've graduated from sheer impatience to a more thoughtful approach.

I chose to make these cushions using a traditional pin-striped blue-and-white cotton fabric, but you could try a much stronger stripe for a more contemporary effect.

The circles print on the piped edging can either be used for the cushion back or, as I have done with these cushions, just employed for the edging on the "envelope" back (see page 97).

how to make the striped cushions

These cushions are made as a pair. On one, the stripes run around and around to form concentric squares, and on the other they radiate out from the center.

You will need enough striped fabric for both cushion fronts and the "envelope" cushion backs, and enough patterned fabric for the piped edging. Piping the edges of the cushions takes a little extra time, but once you have mastered the technique, you can use it on other projects.

materials

For two finished cushions measuring approximately 16in (40cm) square, you will need:
Two 44in (112cm) wide cotton fabrics as follows—
  A = 1¼yd (1.1m) of a narrow stripe (ROWAN *Blue-and-White Stripe* BWS01)
  B = ½yd (45cm) of a small-scale print (ROWAN *Roman Glass* GP01S)
Matching thread
4yd (3.7m) piping cord
Two pillow forms, each 16in (40cm) square

making the patchwork fronts

1 Cut two 18½in (47cm) squares from fabric A, making sure that you are cutting the stripes precisely on the straight grain of the fabric. Then cut one square into quarters, cutting diagonally from corner to corner in each direction to form four triangles. Cut the other square into quarters in the same way. You will see that on four of the eight triangles, the stripes run parallel to the longest side and on the remaining four, the stripes run perpendicular to the longest side. Group the matching triangles together so there are four matching triangles in each set.

2 Now arrange each set of four matching triangles to form squares. The stripes on one set form concentric squares (see below). The stripes on the other set radiate outward from the center (see page 70).

3 With right sides together, pin and machine stitch the triangles of each cushion front to each other, leaving ½in (1.5cm) seam allowances. First join the triangles in pairs (see below), then join the pairs to complete the two patchwork fronts. Press the seams open as you go.

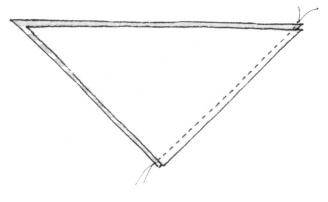

finishing the cushions

1 For covering the piping cord for each cushion, cut out 2¹/₂in (6cm) wide bias strips from fabric B, joining lengths to make a single piece at least 70in (178cm) long. If you have never cut and joined bias strips, see page 20 for full instructions. Press the seams open on the joined strips (see below).

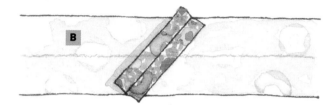

2 Lay the piping cord in the center of the wrong side of the bias strip. Fold the strip over the piping cord and baste the two layers of fabric together close to the cord (see below).

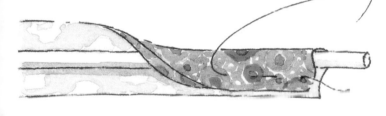

3 For each cushion cover back, cut out two retangles each 17in by 11¹/₂in (43cm by 29cm) from fabric A. Hem and pin the backs together as for the mixed-print cushion in step 2 on page 35.

4 With the right sides together, pin the cushion front to the backs with the piping cord sandwiched in between and all the raw edges aligned, except at the corners where the piping will form a curve. If the piping cord is a fairly thin one, overlap the ends of the covered cord (so that they will be caught in the seam) and clip off the excess ends after the seam has been stitched. If the cord is too thick to do this, trim off the ends the piping cord so they butt up to each other, glue them together where they touch, then fold under the raw edges at the ends of the bias strip and sew them together. Once all the layers are securely pinned in place, baste them together.

Using a piping foot or zipper foot on the machine, machine stitch around the cushion as close to the piping cord as possible (see below). Remove the basting.

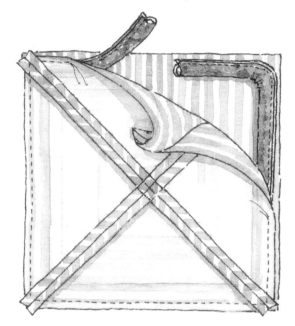

5 Finally, clip V-shaped notches in the seam allowances of all the layers of fabric at the corners of the cushion to ease the piping around the corners (see below). Turn the cover right side out and insert the pillow form.

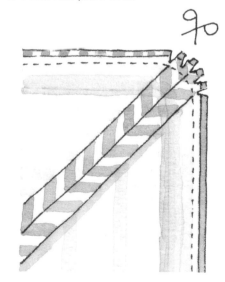

tote bag

I hate plastic shopping bags—not only are they bad for the environment, they also cut into your hands when they are heavy and they seem to breed in the kitchen. This fabric bag folds away neatly, so you could make two or three in different colorways and take them with you when you go to the store.

Really, though, this tote bag is so pretty you will not be able to help using it every time you need to carry a little more than you can fit in your handbag. Make sure that the handles are just long enough to fit over your shoulder if necessary.

Although it barely fits the description of patchwork, the bag follows the principle by using two different fabrics, one for the handles and one for the bag. However, if you prefer a more patched appearance, follow the method used for the table runner on pages 66–69 and create vertical stripes of toning prints for the bag and add plain handles, or make a highly patched version (like the cushion on pages 32–35) if you want a retro look.

how to make the tote bag

This bag is very simple to make. I found it easiest to make up two handles first, attach them to the front and back of the bag, then sew together the bag pieces and the lining. If you wish, you can pad the bag as per the padded shoulder bag on pages 88–91.

materials

For a finished bag measuring 16in (40cm) long by 14in (35cm) wide and a shoulder strap 24in (61cm) long, you will need:

½yd (45cm) of each of three 44in (112cm) wide cotton fabrics as follows—

A = circles print (ROWAN *Roman Glass* GP01J)

B = narrow stripe (ROWAN *Pachrangi Stripe* PS05)

C = lining fabric of your choice

Matching thread

cutting and stitching the bag

1 For the front and back of the bag, cut out two rectangles from fabric A (see below), each 19in by 15in (48cm by 38cm). For the bag handles, cut two strips from fabric B, each 5in (13cm) wide by 54in (137cm) long (piecing for long enough strips). For the lining, cut two pieces from fabric C, each 15in (38cm) square. These pieces all include ½in (1.5cm) seam allowances.

2 Turn under and press 2½in (6.5cm) along the top edge of each fabric-A bag piece. Set aside.

3 Sew the handle pieces into tubes and turn right side out (see page 22). The raw edges at the ends will be caught in the bag seams. Align the seam line with one side edge and press flat.

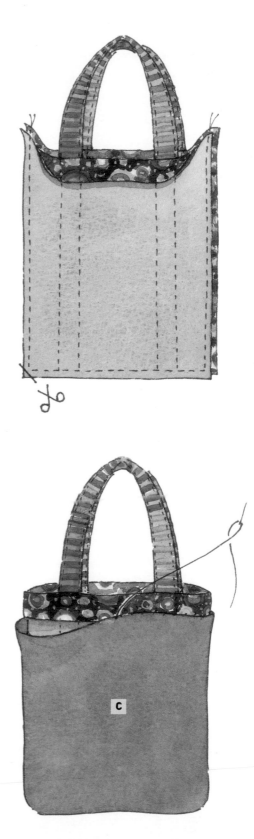

4 Pin and baste a strap to the right side of the front and back of the bag, making sure that they are in the same position on the back and the front. I placed my handles 3¹/₂in (9.5cm) away from the side edges. Topstitch the handles to the bag along each side, continuing the topstitching along the handle (see above).

5 Place both sides of the bag right sides together and pin, unfolding the hem at the sides (see above right) and paying special attention to the bottom of the bag to make sure the straps are aligned. Machine stitch, leaving a ¹/₂in (1.5cm) seam allowance all the way around.

6 Snip off a triangle of the seam allowances at the bottom corners (see above right). Press the seams open under the hem at the top, then fold down the hem again and press.

7 Stitch the lining pieces together as for the bag. Fold under and press ¹/₂in (1.5cm) along the top edge, then slip stitch the lining to the bag (see right). Turn the bag right side out and press.

lavender bags

All my friends seem to use lavender bags nowadays. They smell wonderful, have a lovely nostalgic feel about them, and allegedly keep the moths at bay. I like to use them under the pillows on my bed or in my lingerie drawer, but you can also add a loop (as for the potholder on page 49) and hang them in the closet.

I have employed a simple four-square patch combination that shows how a single striped fabric can be used to create a striking design effect. Stacked up in a pile and tied with pretty ribbon, these bags make a great housewarming present.

You could make a much bigger version as a small cushion (and slip a muslin bag of lavender in with the pillow form) to make a sweet-smelling addition to your living room or bed.

how to make the lavender bags

The front of these lavender bags is made from four little squares pieced together. The back of the bag can be cut from a plain toning fabric or, as here, from the same fabric as the front patches.

I used two vintage buttons, one on each side, to tie the lavender-stuffed bag together at the center. Be sure to take a swatch of your fabric with you when buying buttons.

The Rowan fabric used for these bags has a diagonal stripe, and the little square patches are cut on the straight grain of the fabric. If you are using scraps from you own stash, be sure you use a diagonal stripe if you want to achieve the same effect.

materials

For a finished bag measuring 5½in (14cm), you will need:

Small amount of a 44in (112cm) wide, diagonally striped cotton fabric (ROWAN *Diagonal Poppy* in either GP24BL or GP24LV)

Two small matching buttons

Matching thread

Lavender for stuffing

cutting and stitching the bag

1 First, cut one 6½in (17cm) square for the back of the bag, cutting on the straight grain of the fabric. Then, again cutting on the straight grain of the fabric, cut four 3¾in (10cm) square patches from the diagonal stripe fabric, pattern-matching the corners exactly so that the patches are identical, with the stripes lining up exactly the same way in each of the squares. If the stripes are easy to line up or if you are not concerned about forming exact concentric lines with your striped patches, you will find it quicker to cut a single

piece of fabric first, measuring 7½in (20cm) square, then cut this large square into quarters (see below).

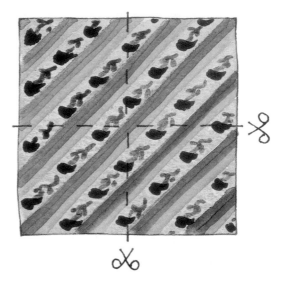

2 Arrange the four small squares so that the stripes match up to form concentric squares (see below), or position them so that the stripes point toward the center (see page 78).

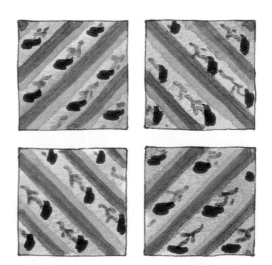

3 Pin and stitch the four squares to each other, with right sides together and leaving ¹/₂in (1.5cm) seam allowances (see below). Press the seams open.

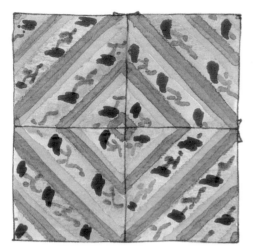

4 Lay the patched front on top of the back piece, with right sides together. Pin and stitch, leaving a ¹/₂in (1.5cm) seam allowance and leaving the top open (see below). To ensure crisp corners, clip off a triangle of the seam allowances at each of the two bottom corners. Turn right side out and press under the seam allowances at the opening.

5 Insert the lavender so that the bag is roughly half full.

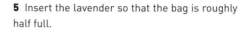

6 Carefully topstitch all around the edges (see below), closing the opening as you go. (It is best to start stitching at the opening end and, with the machine needle left in the fabric, to push the lavender to the other side of the bag as you stitch.)

7 For a decorative touch, add a button to the center of each side of the lavender bag like a quilting tie (see above).

alternative colorways and designs

You can make your lavender bags in different colorways. I chose to make mine using the same Rowan print in different color schemes, but you can also mix and match the prints within each of the bags.

If you want to use up some striped scraps and none of them has diagonal stripes, then cut the patches as for the striped cushions on pages 70–73 and make two bags at once.

I stitched a small matching vintage button in the center of each side of the bags, but a simple quilting tie using a thick embroidery thread also makes a nice finish. Tying quilts is great for simple quilting and a good technique for impatient patchworkers.

This design would work just as well on a larger scale, with striped squares placed at different angles to make a quilt.

notebook cover

I love those pretty fabric-covered books you can buy at stationery stores, but they are often expensive. Plain notebooks are not and covering them yourself makes them much more personal. It's also a great way to use up small scraps leftover from bigger patchwork projects. I have chosen a very simple pieced look, with one printed fabric for the main part of the cover and a plain one for the spine, copying the way books are bound in leather and cloth.

The books shown here are A5-size notebooks, known as quartos, but you can make covers to fit any size of book—how about one for the kitchen for organizing all those loose recipes. The covers are removable so they can be transferred to a new book once the last one is full, and they can also be washed if necessary.

Of course, covered notebooks also make ideal presents. For a commemorative scrapbook, use fabrics leftover from special-occasion dresses.

how to make the notebook cover

The size of the notebook you choose determines the size of the fabric pieces for this cover. Use leftover scraps of your choice, or buy small amounts of the Rowan fabrics listed below for the cover shown on page 84.

materials

For a notebook of your chosen size, you will need:
Small amount of each of two Rowan cottons as follows—
   A = large-scale print (ROWAN *Chard* GP09L)
   B = solid color (ROWAN *Shot Cotton* SC41)
Matching thread
Matching narrow silk ribbon for bookmark (optional)

cutting and stitching the cover

1 To determine the size of your patches, measure the size of the notebook you are covering. First, measure the length of the notebook, then measure around the width from front to back, with the notebook closed. Draw this outline on a large piece of paper and cut out. Then cut a strip out of the center of this paper pattern to the desired width for the spine patch. Trace this center piece again on paper, and add a hem allowance at the top and bottom of 1¼in (4cm) and a seam allowance of ½in (1.5cm) at each side. Use one of the remaining paper pieces to trace the paper pattern for the other two patches. To this pattern piece, add a hem allowance at the top and bottom of 1¼in (4cm), a seam allowance of 1in (3cm) at one side and a wraparound flap of 4½in (11.5cm) at the other side.

2 Cut two pieces from fabric A to the size of the larger paper pattern piece, and cut one piece from fabric B to the size of the smaller paper pattern piece.

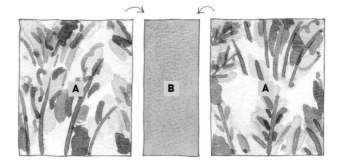

3 Arrange the three fabric patches with the smallest patch in the middle (see above). Then pin and stitch the pieces to each other, with the right sides together and leaving ½in (1.5cm) seam allowances. Press the seams open.

4 Turn under and press ½in (1.5cm) along each end of the pieced patchwork. Then turn under ½in (1.5cm) again to form a double hem. Pin and baste these double hems in position. Pin and baste double hems along the top and bottom in the same way (see below). Topstitch the hems to secure. (If you want a bookmark, before topstitching read step 6). Remove the basting and press.

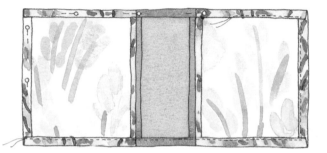

5 Lay your notebook on the cover so that the spine is at the center of the patchwork. Then mark the position of the fold line for the wraparound flaps with pins (see below). Do this at each end of the cover. For symmetry, make sure that the wraparound flaps are the same length at each end so that the fabric-B patch is centered on the spine of the notebook.

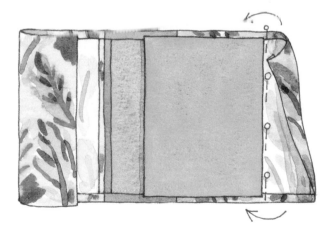

6 Remove the notebook and pin, then baste, the wraparound flaps in place, with right sides together (see below). Slip the cover on the notebook to test the fit and adjust if necessary. Overcast stitch the flaps in place across the top and bottom of each flap (see page 19) and remove the basting.

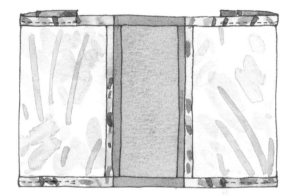

7 Turn the cover right side out and press (see below). For a bookmark, hand sew a length of ribbon to the inside of the cover at the center top. (Alternatively, you could catch the ribbon in the double hem when topstitching in step 4).

padded shoulder bag

This padded shoulder bag will brighten up any outfit. It can be made in any colorway you desire, and is big enough to house everything a girl needs. The straps are long enough to sling over your shoulder, but wide enough so that they feel comfortable on your shoulder if the contents of your bag are heavy.

It has a slightly more feminine shape than the more sturdy tote bag on pages 74–77. If you were feeling somewhat patient, you could quilt the bag to give it an extra *je ne sais quoi*. Follow the instructions for free-motion quilting on page 25, and carry out the quilting as explained on page 92.

The more I look at this bag, the more I think that it is actually an ideal knitting bag. You could carry all your yarn around, and the padding would ensure that you do not harm anyone standing next to you with your knitting needles.

how to make the padded shoulder bag

If you want to carry the bag slung over your shoulder, make sure that the handles are long enough for comfort—the ones here measure 23in by 3in (59cm by 7.5cm) when finished. Test the length with a tape measure, and adjust the length of the handle pieces if required.

materials

For a finished bag measuring 16½in (42cm) long by 15in (38cm) wide, you will need:

Five 44in (112cm) wide cotton fabrics as follows—

A = ½yd (45cm) of a large-scale floral (ROWAN *August Roses* GP18MG)

B = ¼yd (25cm) of a narrow stripe (ROWAN *Alternative Stripe* AS03)

C = ¼yd (25cm) of a solid color (ROWAN *Shot Cotton* SC03)

D = ½yd (45cm) of a second solid color (ROWAN *Shot Cotton* SC47), for handles

E = ½yd (45cm) of lining fabric of your choice

Cotton batting, 36in by 16in (90cm by 41cm)

Matching thread

making the patchwork

1 First, cut out your fabric patches for the front and back of the bag. Cut two rectangles each 10½in by 16in (27cm by 41cm) from floral-fabric A. Cut two strips each 4in by 16in (11cm by 41cm) from stripe-fabric B. Cut two strips each 7in by 16in (18cm by 41cm) from plain-fabric C.

2 For the handles, cut two strips, each 28in by 7in (72cm by 18cm), from plain-fabric D. For the lining, cut two rectangles, each 15½in by 16in (40cm by 41cm), from fabric E. For the batting, cut two pieces, each 17in by 16in (43.5cm by 41cm). Set aside these pieces to use when finishing the bag.

3 With right sides together, pin and machine stitch the patches to each other in the order shown below, leaving ½in (1.5cm) seam allowances. Press the seams open.

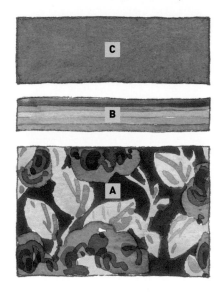

4 Using tailor's chalk or a water-soluble pen and a plate as a template, draw curved lines around the bottom corners of the bag and trim away the curved corners (see below).

finishing the bag

1 Using the bag as a template, trim the bottom corners of each of the batting pieces to the shape of the patched front and back. Pin and/or baste a piece of batting to the wrong side of the back and the front (see below).

2 Fold each handle strip in half lengthwise with right sides together. Leaving a ½in (1.5cm) seam allowance, machine stitch along the long edges to form a tube (see page 22). Turn right side out. Turn inside the ends and press them. Next, mark the position for the bag handles on the front and back of the bag approximately 3in (8cm) from the sides of the bag), and stitch in place, stitching a square and then stitching diagonally across the square to strengthen (see below and page 22). Be sure to catch in the batting, but not the top hem.

3 Pin and baste the back and front to each other, with the right sides together. Machine stitch, leaving a ½in (1.5cm) seam allowance. Trim back the excess batting close to the seam to reduce bulkiness. Fold the top 2½in (6.5cm) of the bag fabric over the batting (see above).

4 Trim and stitch the lining pieces together as for the bag. Turn right side out. Slip the lining over the bag, fold under a ½in (1.5cm) hem at the top, and slip stitch the top of the lining to the bag (see above). Turn the bag right side out and press.

how to make the quilted shoulder bag

This bag is similar to the one on pages 88–91, but here I made it with different fabrics, then quilted the bag using two different techniques—straight lines across the top and a free-motion pattern over the bottom (see pages 23–25).

materials

For a finished bag measuring 16½in (42cm) long by 15in (38cm) wide, you will need:
Five 44in (112cm) wide cotton fabrics as follows—
   A = ½yd (45cm) of a large-scale floral (ROWAN *Dahlia* MN06RD)
   B = ¼yd (25cm) of a narrow stripe (ROWAN *Pachrangi Stripe* PS05)
   C = ¼yd (25cm) of a solid color (ROWAN *Shot Cotton* SC22)
   D = ½yd (45cm) of a second solid color (ROWAN *Shot Cotton* SC33) for handles
   E = 1yd (90cm) of lining fabric of your choice
Cotton batting, 36in by 16in (90cm by 41cm)
Matching thread

making the bag

1 For the front and back of the bag, cut two rectangles, each 10½in by 16in (27cm by 41cm), from floral-fabric A, two strips, each 4in by 16in (11cm by 41cm), from stripe-fabric B, and two strips, each 7in by 16in (18cm by 41cm), from plain-fabric C.

2 Following step 2 for the padded bag on page 90, cut out the handle pieces (fabric D), the lining (fabric E), and the batting. Set aside these pieces to use when finishing the bag.

3 Following steps 3 and 4 for the padded bag on page 90, prepare the front and back patchworks.

4 Pin the batting in place as for step 1 on page 91. Then cut two extra pieces of lining to the size of the batting, position them over the batting, and baste or spray glue the layers together (see pages 23–25).

5 Using the quilting foot on the sewing machine, quilt the top of the bag with straight horizontal lines (see above).

6 Free-motion quilt the flowers (see above), using a darning foot on the machine and loosely following the petal outlines.

7 Finish as for the shoulder bag on page 91 in steps 2–4.

checkerboard cushion

This cushion has a vintage air about it, and that is what makes it so charming. It looks best in a group, made in a series of contrasting colorways, to go on a bed, sofa, or large chair, and looks best in bold colors that contrast with its setting. You could make a different colored cushion for each kitchen chair in the toning blues of the tablecloth on page 52, as the piecing system is the same here.

The patterned squares of the patchwork for these cushions could be cut from random prints—a perfect way to use up scraps leftover from other patchwork projects. You could use also use striped fabric to replace some of the plain squares (see pages 98 and 99).

If the fabric you are using is quite thin, it is a good idea to line the cushion front before sewing on the back. With the patched seams covered, the cover will be more durable and will withstand frequent washing. The cushions shown here have a simple "envelope" back, and you could add a nice finishing detail there by creating a contrasting border along the "envelope" edge.

how to make the checkerboard cushion

Make the central patchwork part of the cushion front first, then add the borders. Finally, prepare the back pieces and join all the parts of the cushion cover.

materials

For a finished cushion measuring 16in (40cm) square, you will need:

Two 44in (112cm) wide cotton fabrics as follows –

  A = ¼yd (25cm) of a small-scale floral (ROWAN *Kashmir* GP-BK or GP25GY)

  B = 1yd (90cm) of a solid color (ROWAN *Shot Cotton* SC45 or SC41)

Matching thread

Pillow form, 16in (40cm) square

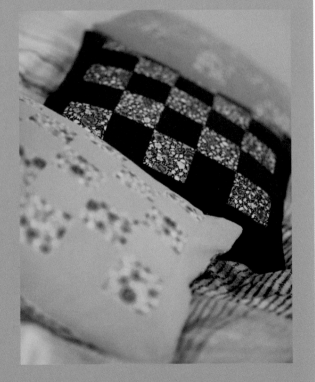

cutting and stitching the cover

1 For the central patchwork, cut thirteen 3in (7.2cm) squares from fabric A and twelve from fabric B—for a total of twenty-five squares.

2 Arrange the twenty-five patches in five rows of five patches, alternating the plain and patterned squares to form a checkerboard design.

3 Take the first two patches of the first row and pin and machine stitch them to each other, with right sides together and leaving a ¼in (6mm) seam allowance (see below top). Press the seam open (see below bottom). Join the remaining patches into a total of five rows of five patches.

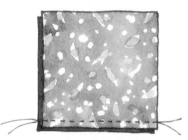

4 To complete the central patchwork, sew together the five-patch rows (see below), pressing the seams open as you go.

5 For the borders, cut four strips 2¹/₂in (7.2cm) wide from fabric B—two 13in (31.2cm) long and two 17in (43cm) long. Leaving ¹/₄in (6mm) seam allowances, sew the shorter strips to the top and bottom of the patchwork and the longer ones to the sides (see below). Press the seams open as you go.

6 Using fabric B for the cushion back, cut out, hem, sew on the two back pieces, and finish as for the back of the same-size cushion in steps 1–4 on page 35 (see below).

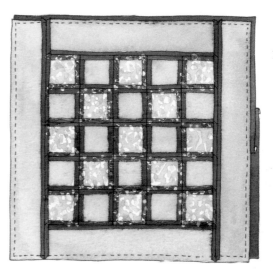

cushion back alternative

For an extra decorative touch, before sewing on the cushion backs you can add a contrasting border to the outer back piece. Simply cut a binding strip 4in (10cm) wide from the contrasting fabric. Stitch the binding to the outer opening back piece, with right sides together and stitching 1in (2.5cm) from the edge. Press 1in (2.5cm) under along the free edge of the binding, then fold it over the back fabric and sew in place.

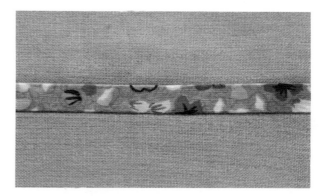

alternative variations

These variations on the checkerboard design are made using the same piecing technique as the checkerboard cushion. The cushion on the left has a more organized pattern, in which stripes, florals, and plain fabrics form a loose checkerboard effect.

The patch format on the cushion below is much more random, and I have chosen here to use a painterly palette of toning colors from a wider range of quite different floral prints. These two cushions demonstrate what the fun of designing patchwork is all about: from a very simple, basic design tool, you can create a range of marvelously diverse effects.

Try creating similar design variations of your own. You could base a quilt on the cushion design below, with the squares each several times larger than these and with the addition of a proportionally wider border.

makeup bag

It is fun to have lovely little things made out of patchwork that you can use every day. Makeup bags are so simple to stitch, and yet we often settle for a freebie that we get when we buy cosmetics. Make one yourself and you can really express your personality in the colors and prints you pick and, of course, the way you put them together. Once you have sewn one, it will be even easier to stitch a few more as presents for friends.

I made this makeup bag from a mixture of striped and floral cotton fabrics in toning oranges and yellows, padded it with cotton batting, and lined it with a bright, solid-colored fabric. Putting in a zipper can take a little extra time, but once you have mastered the technique, you can make zippered cushions, or translate this bag into a bigger one with a zipper and handles (see the shoulder bag on pages 88–91).

how to make the makeup bag

This bag has three-dimensional corners, so it will sit upright on a shelf or by the sink. The zipper is easy to insert, as it is added before the back and front are joined.

materials

For a finished makeup bag measuring approximately 8¹/₂in (22cm) across the top, 6in (15.5cm) long, and with a base 2in by 6¹/₂in (5cm by 17cm), you will need:
Small amount of each of three cotton fabrics as follows—
  A = narrow stripe (ROWAN *Pachrangi Stripe* PS13)
  B = medium-scale floral (ROWAN *Flower Lattice* GP11C)
  C = lining fabric of your choice
Matching thread
Cotton batting, 10in by 24in (25cm by 60cm)
8in (20cm) zipper

making the front and back

1 For the patches for the front and back of the bag, cut two pieces from fabric A, each 3in by 9¹/₂in (8cm by 25cm), and two pieces, each 4¹/₂in by 9¹/₂in (12cm by 25cm); then cut two pieces from fabric B, each 2¹/₂in by 9¹/₂in (7cm by 25cm). For the lining, cut two pieces of fabric C, each 8in by 9¹/₂in (21cm by 25cm). Cut two pieces of batting, each 7¹/₂in by 9¹/₂in (19.5cm by 25cm). Set aside the lining and batting to use when finishing the bag.

2 To make the front of the makeup bag, take one patch of each size (a small fabric-A patch, a big fabric-A patch, and a fabric-B patch). Arrange these three patches with the small fabric-A patch at the top, the big fabric-A patch at the bottom, and the fabric-B patch in between. Pin and machine stitch these pieces to each other, with right sides together and leaving ¹/₂in (1.5cm) seam allowances.

Then press the seams open. Make the back of the bag in the same way as the front (see below).

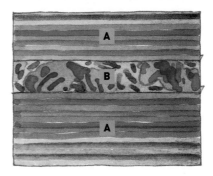

padding and lining the bag

1 Turn under ¹/₂in (1.5cm) along the top edge on both the front and back patchworks and press. Pin the zipper between the back and the front (see below), with the

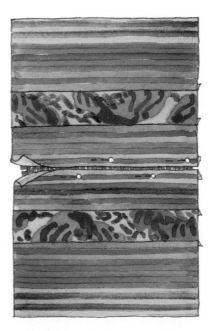

folded edges along the zipper teeth and the zipper on the wrong side. Baste the zipper in place and machine stitch.

2 Position the two pieces of batting on the wrong side of the bag back and front, with the top edge of the batting aligned with the edges of the zipper tape. Slip stitch the top of the batting to the bottom edges of the zipper tape to secure it (see below). This hand stitching does not have to be neat—it will not be seen—but it does have to be secure.

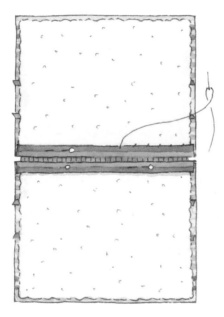

3 Fold the bag right sides together, leaving the zipper slightly open. Pin around the sides, aligning the patch seams. Stitch around the bag, leaving a ½in (1.5cm) seam allowance and tapering a little at the top to meet the zipper (see below).

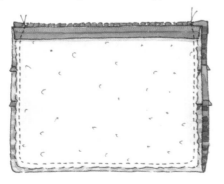

4 Trim back any excess batting close to the side and bottom seams.

5 To shape the corners of the bag, pull each corner flat by pinching the side and bottom seams together. (The formation of the corners is illustrated without the batting so that you can see more clearly how to do it.) Machine stitch across each corner, about 1in (2.5cm) from the corner point. Cut off the surplus triangles of fabric ¼in (6mm) from the seam (see below).

6 To make the bag lining, join the two pieces of lining by pinning and stitching the sides and bottom. Shape the lining corners as for the bag and turn right side out. Slip the lining over the bag while it is still inside out, turn under a hem at the top, and slip stitch the top of the lining to the bag (see below). Turn the bag right side out.

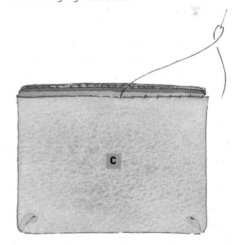

useful terms

*Backstitch Series of small hand stitches in which the thread is taken back over the stitch just made to create strong seams.

Basting Long running stitches used to hold two pieces of fabric together temporarily before they are machine stitched together.

Bias In fabric terminology, the 45-degree angle to the straight grain. Fabrics cut on the bias (i.e., at this angle) are stretchy.

Bias binding Strips of bias-cut fabrics used for border edgings because they will stretch around corners.

Darning foot Special circular sewing-machine foot used for free-motion quilting or embroidery.

Feed dogs The teeth on the sewing plate of a sewing machine. Used to grip the fabric as it is stitched.

Miter A corner in which two pieces of fabric are brought together at a 45-degree angle. Most frequently used on fabric borders.

*Overcast stitch (also known as whipping stitch or oversewing) Hand stitch used to stitch the edges of fabric together.

Pinking shears Scissors with serrated blades, used to prevent fabric edges from fraying.

Quilting Stitching of two or more fabrics together by hand or machine.

Quilting foot Special sewing-machine foot used for quilting.

Quilting pins Extra-long pins specially made for holding layers of fabric together.

Rotary cutter Wheel-type blade used for rapid and accurate cutting of fabric for patchwork.

*Running stitch Series of small, regular hand stitches gathered onto the needle as you stitch. Often used to gather fabric or for hand basting.

Selvage (selvedge) The edges of a length of fabric, which are woven so that the fabric threads cannot unravel.

*Slip stitch Small hand stitches used to join fabrics together invisibly. Useful for hemming.

*Stab stitch Straight hand stitches made by inserting the needle perpendicularly through the fabric; each insertion of the needle is made separately. Used for stitching thick fabrics together and as an embroidery stitch.

Straight grain The grain of the fabric that runs parallel to either the warp or weft threads.

Straight stitch The standard stitch used in sewing machines that forms a straight line of stitches by drawing thread from the top of the machine (the cotton reel) through the needle, the bottom (the bobbin), and the sewing plate.

Template Paper, cardboard, or plastic pattern used as a guide for cutting fabric pieces to the same size and shape.

Tone The lightness or darkness of a color determined by the quantity of black in its makeup.

Warp The threads in a piece of fabric that have been stretched lengthwise in the loom. They run parallel to the selvages.

Weft The cross threads woven into the warp threads to make the fabric. They run perpendicular to the selvages.

Zigzag stitch A sewing machine stitch in which the needle swings from left to right to form a zigzagged line.

*See page 19 for how to work these hand stitches.

templates and patterns

HEXAGON, DIAMOND, AND TRIANGLE TEMPLATES

The two hexagon templates below are for the coasters on pages 58–59, and the diamond and triangle templates on the opposite page are for the star mats on pages 60–61. Use the smaller template of each shape to cut the paper patterns (one paper for each patch) and the larger template to cut the fabric patches. The template for the fabric patches includes the seam allowance—the solid line is the seam line, and the broken line is the cutting line. When cutting the fabric

patches, line up the arrow with the straight grain of the fabric (parallel or perpendicular to the selvage).

APRON PATTERN PIECES

The diagram below shows the sizes to cut the main piece and the pockets for the apron on pages 62–65. Cut all the pieces on the straight grain of the fabric.

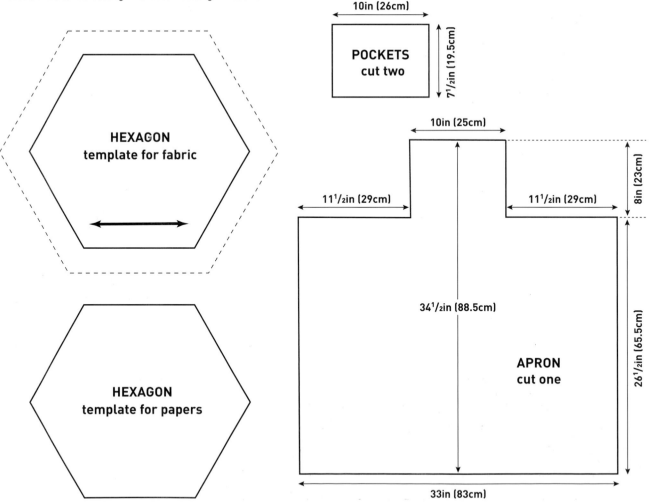

HEXAGON
template for fabric

HEXAGON
template for papers

10in (26cm)

POCKETS
cut two

7¹/₂in (19.5cm)

10in (25cm)

8in (23cm)

11¹/₂in (29cm)

11¹/₂in (29cm)

34¹/₂in (88.5cm)

26¹/₂in (65.5cm)

APRON
cut one

33in (83cm)

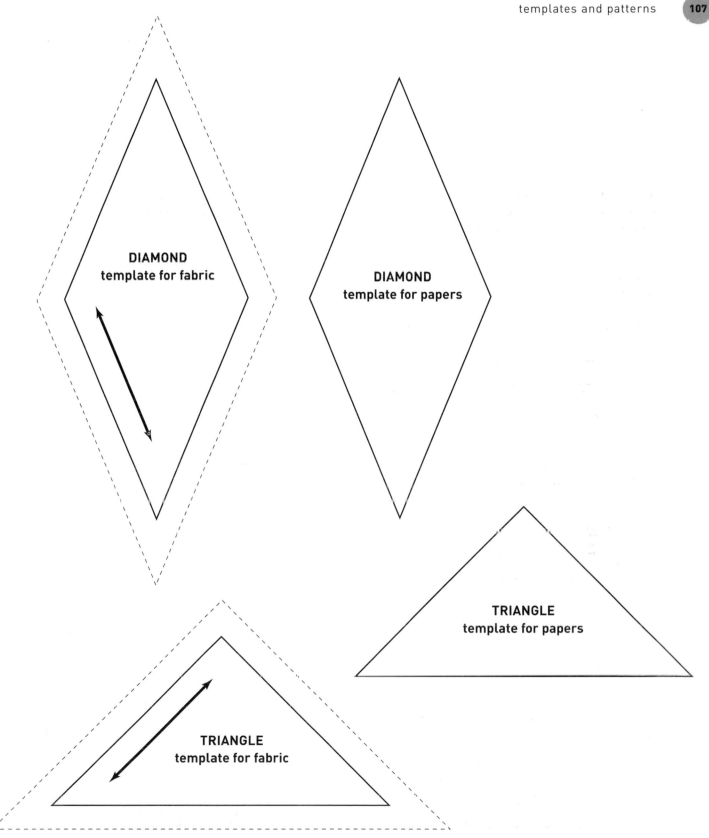

DIAMOND
template for fabric

DIAMOND
template for papers

TRIANGLE
template for papers

TRIANGLE
template for fabric

fabric information

The Kaffe Fassett fabrics used throughout this book are all from the Kaffe Fassett Collection by Rowan in 100 percent pure cotton. The width is approximately 45in (114cm).

All fabric should be washed before use to ensure that there is no uneven shrinkage and no bleeding of colors in later laundering. Press the fabric while it is still damp to return it to its natural crispness.

ABOUT THE KAFFE FASSETT COLLECTION FABRICS

These fabrics were all specially designed for patchworkers by Kaffe Fassett, one of the foremost colorists and most noted patchworkers of his day, and by select designers whose work has been chosen by him.

Kaffe's aim was to create a wide range of exciting designs that would complement each other across many of the patterns and colors, so the collection includes both plain fabrics (shot cottons), geometric designs (stripes and checks), and large bold patterns as well as small repeating patterns.

The Kaffe Fassett fabric collection grows each year, as a new design, usually in a series of half a dozen colors, is added, and some colors and patterns, inevitably, are dropped to make way for them. However, the collection has been designed with a unique color balance that works across many of the design ranges, so it should be easy to find substitute patterns and colors where necessary.

To order the Kaffe Fassett fabrics, please contact the distributors at the addresses provided here to find the stockist nearest you (where there is not a distributor in a country, the nearest one is listed). The fabrics have names and color numbers to identify them; please use these when ordering fabrics. Resources for other fabric suppliers have also been included.

fabrics

Distributors for Rowan's Kaffe Fassett collection for USA and Canada

Westminster Fibers Inc.
4 Townsend West
Suite 8
Nashua
NH 03063
Tel: 603 886 5041
E-mail: rowan@westminsterfibers.com

Other fabric resources

Hancock Fabrics, Inc.
One Fashion Way
Baldwyn
MS 38824
Tel: 877-322-7427
www.hancockfabrics.com

Michael's Fabrics
4 Sandview Court
Baltimore
MD 21209
Tel: 877-266-8918

New England Fabrics
55 Ralston Street
Keene
NH 03431
Tel: 603-352-8683

sewing and embroidery threads

Coats & Clark
4135 South Stream Boulevard
Charlotte
North Carolina 28217
Tel: 704 329 5016

Madeira
30 Bayside Court
Laconia
NH 03246
Tel: 800-225-3001

Sulky of America
P.O.Box 49412
Port Charlotte
FL 33949-4129
Tel: 800-874-4115
Fax: 941-743-4634
E-mail: info@sulky.com

Distributors for Rowan's Kaffe Fassett collection in other countries

AUSTRALIA
XLN Fabrics
2/21 Binney Road
Kings Park
NEW SOUTH WALES 2148
Tel: 61 2 96213066

BELGIUM
Rhinetex
Geurdeland 7
6673 DR ANDELST
HOLLAND
Tel: 31 488 480030

DENMARK
Industrial Textiles
Engholm Parkvej 1
DK 3450 ALLERØD
Tel: 45 48 17 20 55
E-mail: mail@indutex.dk

FINLAND
Coats Upti UY
Ketjutie 3
04220 KERAVA
Tel: 358 9 274 871
E-mail: coatsoptisales@coats.com

FRANCE
Rhinetex
Geurdeland 7
6673 DR ANDELST
HOLLAND
Tel: 31 488 480030

GERMANY
Rhinetex
Geurdeland 7
6673 DR ANDELST
HOLLAND
Tel: 31 488 480030

HOLLAND
Rhinetex
Geurdeland 7
6673 DR ANDELST
Tel: 31 488 480030

ICELAND
Storkurinn
Laugavegi 59
101 REYKJAVIK
Tel: 354 551 8258
E-mail: malin@mmedia.is

ITALY
DL SRL
Via Piave 24-26
20016 PERO
MILANO
Tel: 39 02 339 10 180

JAPAN
Yokota & Co. Ltd.
5-14 2 Chome Minamikyuhoojimachi
Chuo-Ku
OSAKA
Tel: 81 6 6251 7179

NEW ZEALAND
Fabco Limited
P.O. Box 84-002
Westgate
AUCKLAND 1250
Tel: 64 9 411 9996

NORWAY
Industrial Textiles
Engholm Parkvej 1
DK 3450 ALLERØD
DENMARK
Tel: 45 48 17 20 55
E-mail: mail@indutex.dk
Fax: (82) 2 521 5181

SOUTH AFRICA
Arthur Bales PTY Ltd.
PO Box 44644
LINDEN 2104
Tel: 27 11 888 2401

SPAIN
Lucretia Beleta Patchwork
Dr Rizal 12
08006 BARCELONA
Tel: 34 93 41 59555

SWITZERLAND
Rhinetex
Geurdeland 7
6673 DR ANDELST
HOLLAND
Tel: 31 488 480030

SWEDEN
Industrial Textiles
Engholm Parkvej 1
DK 3450 ALLERØD
DENMARK
Tel: 45 48 17 20 55
E-mail: mail@indutex.dk

TAIWAN
Long Teh Trading Co.
3F No 19-2
Kung Yuan Road
TAICHUNG
Tel: 886 4 2225 6698

UK
Rowan Yarns
Green Lane Mill
Holmfirth
HD9 2DX
E-mail: mail@knitrowan.com

index

acknowledgments

AUTHOR'S ACKNOWLEDGMENTS
I would like to thank everyone involved in making this book happen, in particular Susan Berry for her tireless hard work, vision, and help. I would also like to thank John Heseltine for his wonderful photography. A big thank-you to Carol Shackleton for inspiring me to take up a career in textiles even though I was always impatient, and for constantly supporting me throughout my career and, indeed, throughout this book. I would like to thank my family for all their love and support. Finally, thanks to James for all his creative input and honesty.

PUBLISHERS' ACKNOWLEDGMENTS
The publishers would like to thank Anne Wilson for her design, John Heseltine for his photography, Carrie Hill for her artworks, Sally Harding for her editorial work, Pauline Smith for her technical advice, Ann Hinchcliffe for her support, and Marie Lorimer for the index.